THE WOOLY

11 Barclay Street, New York, NY 10007
- contact@thewooly.com
- www.thewooly.com
- Opening hours vary
- Transport: 2 and 3 trains/Park Pl; N and R trains/City Hall
- Moderate

> **Creative club in the Woolworth Building "not open since 2009"**

The Wooly, a bar and event space hidden in the first floor of the landmarked Woolworth Building, is as much a testament to the creative spirit of New York City today as the building is a celebration of the technical prowess of the skyscraper era.

Built out of an unused space next to the Woolworth Tower Kitchen restaurant, The Wooly is run by a brother-in-law duo whose personal collection of vintage items from all over the country spills over into the bar they run. From shabby-chic couches from grandmothers they know to light sconces from the Plaza Hotel, The Wooly has the feeling of a place that has been lived in. With old books, stacks of vintage suitcases, a non-functional pipe organ, old radios, simple chandeliers and authentic period wallpaper, it has the makings of a Wes Anderson set, but better because you get to party in it. Many art pieces were commissioned for the space, including a wooly mammoth painting by the co-owner's mother.

To be clear, The Wooly isn't open like a regular bar. The owners joke that they've been "not open since 2009." For the most part, the space hosts events, parties, and creative panel discussions. Thom Yorke and Nigel Godrich did a set at a party for Rag & Bone. Lana Del Rey sang for an H&M event. There have also been sweet sixteens, engagements, and it's a favorite location for parties by architecture studios, art galleries, and design firms. The cocktail menu is deliberately non-fussy, but with fresh ingredients.

This doesn't mean that the ordinary layperson can't get in. If you send an email through their website saying you'll be in town, and they happen to be open, they'll gladly accommodate you. Even for a group of two. "Just hit us up," they say.

Heavy velvet curtains and a painted swan motif block the glass window on the street, but you'll see a small sign on the door and a "W" insignia. This reference to Woolworth is repeated on the floor mosaics inside.

The Woolworth Building was designed to have a ground-floor arcade of shops and restaurants, but it has been a long time since the spaces have been activated. The owners intend The Wooly to be a New York institution, just like the Woolworth Building itself. The event-oriented usage has allowed them to make a visit to The Wooly always a momentous occasion.

The Wooly is one of the most unique bars in New York City—just don't show up at the door unplanned.

ARCADE BAKERY

220 Church Street, New York, NY 10013
- www.arcadebakery.com
- Monday to Friday 8 am – 4 pm
- Transport: 1, 2 and 3 trains/Chambers St
- Moderate

"

French fare in a Tribeca office

For connoisseurs of French bread and pastries, this understated bakery hidden inside a 1920s Tribeca office building is one of the best and most authentic in the city. The beautiful, barrel-vaulted office entrance where Arcade Bakery is located was decommissioned when Gap became the main tenant of the building and wanted a private entrance to their offices. The space was empty for five years until Roger Gural, a self-proclaimed "bread romantic" from Staten Island, decided to open Arcade Bakery. It's a perfect spot for Gural, who wants to give New Yorkers a chance to rediscover the magic of fresh bread, just like in Europe.

With the affordable space at Arcade Bakery, Gural can focus on making fresh products throughout the day, starting at five in the morning until about one in the afternoon. He wants the bread to be made as close as possible to when the customers will consume it.

Gural used to work in television, but started baking bread at home for fun. When he heard that the French Culinary Institute in New York City was offering a new course just on breadmaking, he went all in. While there, David Bouley came for a visit and announced that he was looking for bakers at Bouley Bakery. Gural applied and got the job. Through a connection at Bouley, he went to Paris to work at Au Duc de La Chapelle bakery for award-winning baker Thierry Meunier and then to Le Fournil Borriglione in Nice. When he was ready to open up his own place, the Tribeca location was a no-brainer—Gural's family manages the property where the disused hallway is and he lived in the superintendent's apartment for two years.

About halfway down the entranceway, wooden alcoves come with fold-down tables for customers. Gural, in partnership with Workstead in Gowanus, transformed former display cases into seating and tables. Simultaneously beautiful and clever, the aesthetic was a result of necessary adaptation—the floor of the hallway is sloped. Gural works the register himself, with the bakery built into the wall near the end of the hallway. The bread selection includes classics like baguettes, a round *miche*, *pain d'épi* and *pain au levain*, plus more unique options like pear and buckwheat or a caramel apple brioche. Then there are the many types of babka, like whiskey pecan, *Speculoos*, and chocolate walnut.

For the lunchgoers and the American crowds, there is a lot to choose from. Sandwiches on baguettes include ham with *Comté* cheese, turkey mozzarella, and vegetarian. There are quiches and finally the famous pizzas, so popular you can now advance order online through the Arcade Bakery website and pick up in 15 minutes.

In the end, part of Gural's mission, beyond re-educating New Yorkers about fresh bread, is to help others open their own fresh bread bakeries. "Everyone is a baker," he says and he hopes his staff of four will open their own shops one day. He cross-trains his staff so they know how to work both front and back of house, teaching them everything they need to know to run a bakery. And he's also back at the French Culinary Institute (now the International Culinary Center), teaching the art of breadmaking.

APOTHEKE

9 Doyers Street, New York, NY 10013
212-406-0400
• www.apothekenyc.com
• Open seven days a week 6:30 pm – 2 am
• Transport: J, M, Q and Z trains/Canal St
• Moderate

Apothecary-themed speakeasy

Doyers Street in Chinatown was once called "The Bloody Angle" because the curvilinear road enabled gangs to creep up on one another unseen. Today, at that precise bend of the street is an apothecary-themed speakeasy, aptly named Apotheke. Located in a space formerly occupied by a karaoke and dumpling bar, the only sign that marks the location says "Chemist." The perpetually gated windows are filled with medicinal jars, while an imposing European oak door has a small eyehole. Inside, the bar opens up onto a spectacular old-world inspired space. Above a reclaimed wood floor intermixed with porcelain tiles, the original tin ceiling was discovered under two feet of soundproofing during renovation.

The bartenders wear lab coats (except on Prohibition Wednesdays), serving up a seasonally changing menu with a holistic, "farm to bar" approach above an illuminated bar made from Carrera marble. As such, the ingredients come from New York City greenmarkets, organic vendors, and their own rooftop garden, along with local Chinatown markets and shops. The cocktail menu is organized into sections referencing medicinal remedies like painkillers, stimulants, aphrodisiacs, stress relievers, and euphoric enhancers—liquid prescriptions, essentially. There is also absinthe, prepared the traditional way with sugar and ice-water drip, house-infused cocktail pitchers, and a selection of wines and champagne. Because of the constantly evolving menu, the bartenders get a chance to create new drinks that can be elected to the menu.

Pharmaceutical references are embedded throughout the decor. The chandelier and light fixtures are actually chemistry beakers filled with absinthe. Antique medicine bottles, collected from around the world, are filled with items like phosphoric acid and mustard seed. The wall pattern features a play on the Greek medicinal symbol as well as the organic chemistry of herbs and elixirs. Nods to the Prohibition era are also present throughout–a vintage alcohol still is transformed into the spout for the bathroom sink while an industrial sugarcane press sits in a corner.

Behind the banquette seats you may notice alcoves and archways in the exposed brick wall. These were the original windows of the building, with the bottom half of the openings now buried under landfill. It gives you a sense of how much of the land has been filled in Chinatown and why the rumors of hidden tunnels still persist. In fact, just next door is the entrance to one of those tunnels that enabled some gang escapes in the early 20th century. Enter the tunnel on Doyers Street and pop out in Chatham Square after walking through a fascinating little world of feng shui, reflexology shops, law firms, and travel agencies.

ATTABOY

134 Eldridge Street, New York, NY 10002
- Open daily 6 pm – 4 am
- Transport: B and D trains/Grand St
- Moderate

> *New York's most legitimate speakeasy*

When Sasha Petraske moved Milk & Honey to its Flatiron location, two of his protégés, Michael McIlroy and Sam Ross, set up Attaboy in its place. It might be the most legitimate speakeasy in New York right now. There's no phone. There's no website. When you find the address, all you see on the door is "AB 134. Please Knock Gently." Next to the door, there's a small doorbell with the prompt "Ring Buzzer," as if it was an apartment. Look up and above the door you'll see a closed-circuit camera. Inside, the host and bartenders can see you on a small TV screen behind the bar without relying on the old Prohibition-era peephole. Here, the camera sees all. Don't bother trying to open the door because it's locked. You have to wait for the host to swing open the door, look you over, and decide if he has room for you or not. This may seem terribly pretentious, but with such a tiny space, they simply can't allow overcrowding.

Inside, the place looks much like it did when it was Milk & Honey. The interior is about the width of a train car, with a long narrow bar taking up the front, and a few booths in back, lit (though just barely) by spherical pendant lamps. The whole place can only fit about forty people, with a maximum of eighteen in the booths. The walls are exposed brick. The window facing the street is frosted over, so from the outside you can't see in, but from the inside you can see a faint light filtering in and old lettering.

The booths offer enough privacy that you can focus exclusively on the people you've come with. The best seat, however, is right at the bar, close to the bartenders. Only a couple of bartenders can squeeze back there at a time, but they manage to stir and shake enough cocktails to keep everybody happy. There's no menu, but the bartenders have a thorough enough repertoire of classic cocktails (and variations on the classics) to keep anybody guessing no matter how many drinks they've had and how many times they've been there. They don't stock vodka, but if you don't know that and you ask for it, they'll politely steer you toward gin, and that could go in any number of directions. The Diamond Fizz, a take on the classic Gin Fizz, is concocted from gin, lemon, egg whites whipped into a frothy foam, and champagne.

All the cocktails are prepared with as much thought and dedication as at any other bar in the Milk & Honey school. Yet at the end of the day, these guys are very down to earth. You get the feeling you could talk to them for hours—and maybe you do. The bar is open until 4 am every night, and late nights tend to become a who's who in New York City's cocktail bar scene. Many of the bartenders from the other venues included in this book list Attaboy as their favorite hidden bar.

DARK DISCO AT 88 PALACE

88 East Broadway, New York, NY 10002
- www.facebook.com/DiscoverDarkDisco
- Transport: F train/East Broadway
- $15 – $25

*Dim sum
by day,
nightclub
by night*

Every day until 8 pm, 88 Palace is one of those enormous Chinatown restaurants where dim sum circulates around on rolling carts. But every few months, it becomes a massive dance party after hours run by the organization Dark Disco. The DJs rotate and so does the crowd, but Dark Disco aims to please. As they state, "Dark Disco is committed to partying with a good sound system, lots of shots and a venue with shady corners, where you can love and hate equally and then drink and dance it off."

Situated in a mall directly beneath the Manhattan Bridge, 88 Palace is in that part of Chinatown that never seems to change—it's so noisy, it's hard to imagine that gentrification would come this way (but it probably will). Going to a dance party at 88 Palace is a real trip, from the moment you step into the multi-level East Broadway Mall, which serves as a functional destination for Fuzhou immigrants who come here for employment agencies, prepaid debit cards, and the buses that take workers between restaurants in the city.

During party hours, a bouncer checks identification just inside the mall at street level, attempting to corral partygoers to him. "This is New York," he says when they seem confused about the ID check. There's a lot of hanging out on this first floor and some impromptu dancing. Head up the stairs in the middle of the mall to get checked-in and handed a paper bracelet. There, you'll come upon the red and gold entrance to the dim sum restaurant. It'll be dark and music will be thumping loudly from inside. Normally, the circular restaurant opens up to a central atrium with the escalators of the mall and a large chandelier, but most of this view is curtained off during parties.

Make your way all the way to the front stage area where the DJs are spinning in front of a backdrop of red curtains and gold dragons. It'll be hot and sweaty up here. Smokey too, as the smell of that recently decriminalized drug wafts through the air pungently.

The parties at 88 Palace take place every few months, but you'll need to follow Dark Disco on Facebook to stay in the loop of when they will happen exactly. Make sure to check which DJs are spinning as the style will vary greatly. What's sure is that you'll hear the latest sounds coming out of the electronic/ dance/experimental music scene from all around the world.

PULQUERIA

11 Doyers Street, New York, NY 10013
- 212-227-3099
- www.pulquerianyc.com
- Open Monday to Saturday 6 pm – 2 am
- Transport: J, N, Q, Z and 6 trains/Canal St
- Moderate to expensive

> *Mexican pulque bar in a Chinatown basement*

On Doyers Street (the narrow curving lane off the Bowery where the original gangs of New York held court), most restaurant signs are a mix of Chinese and English. Look for the doorway with the cerulean and white zig-zag pattern, next to Nom Wah Tea Parlor, one of Chinatown's oldest dim sum spots, continually operating since 1920.

Descend the stairs and you'll find a bar on the left and the dining room on the right. Stepping into the warm, dimly lit restaurant with its cerulean and white tiles, copper table tops, and grass mats, you would never know that there was once a Vietnamese restaurant that illegally joined the two spaces. "Everything was held together by chewing gum and chicken wire," owner Christopher Tierney told us. He and his sister Heather bought the place and completed a gut renovation that took nearly two years. They opened Pulqueria in 2011, three years after debuting Apotheke, their turn of the century apothecary-themed cocktail bar two doors down.

Pulqueria and Apotheke share the same clientele, but that's where their similarities end. When Chris and Heather decided to open Pulqueria, they traveled to Mexico City to find inspiration, and brought back some unique finds. Look around and you'll see lots of geometric shapes, colored tiles, and brass fixtures. Grass mats from Mexico cover the ceiling, teal feathers adorn the canopy over the bar, and cinder blocks form room dividers. Tierney brought back pottery from Mexico, painted Aztec-inspired designs onto the tables in the dining room, and fixed up a vintage bar sign found at a street market in Mexico City.

But the most important thing the brother-and-sister team brought back from Mexico was the inspiration for the menu. The restaurant takes its name from *pulque*, a spirit made from fermented agave nectar. "Older than tequila, stronger than beer," Tierney explained. The Aztecs drank *pulque*, and today pulquerias all over Mexico serve it, but it's extremely rare in New York City. Taken straight up, it tastes a bit sour. For something a bit more palatable, try the *curados—pulque* mixed with tequila or mezcal and fresh fruit like mango, tamarind, or coconut. They pair well with the tapas-style menu of light bites, like the ceviches and tuna tostada, served with avocado, chipotle mayo, and crispy onion. "Don't fill up on the guacamole," Tierney warns.

THE SHIP

158 Lafayette Street, New York, NY 10013
- 212-219-8496
- www.theshipnyc.com
- Open Monday to Wednesday 6 pm – 1 am; Thursday to Saturday 6 pm – 3 am
- Transport: J, N, Q, R, Z and 6 trains/Canal St
- Moderate

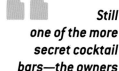

> *Still one of the more secret cocktail bars—the owners would like to keep it that way*

From outside, The Ship looks like a somewhat grungy, perhaps abandoned building, save for the small gold sea monster motif on the door. Coming in off the street, you traverse a long hallway leading to a staircase that goes down into the bar, with a small balcony off to the side where you can see the space below. For a basement, it feels surprisingly large, thanks to the 19-foot tall ceiling. The design is simple and tasteful, with brick walls painted gray, a worn copper bar, and many reclaimed elements. The booths are covered in old sails from a California yacht club, Saarinen chairs are upholstered in U.S. Navy blankets, and a huge light installation in the middle of the room is made of recycled ship parts brought over from Belgium. The stairs are made with wood from the space's original floor, and the cedar planks lining the balcony were taken from old water tanks, ubiquitous on New York City rooftops. Behind the bar, glass windows look out onto a stone wall—common to many buildings in the area. In the evening, when the space is dimly lit by the ceiling fixtures and candles on the tables, the stone wall seems to glow with light coming up from below.

"The Ship started as a venture of friendship," says co-owner Steve Choo, a graphic designer by trade. Back in the late nineties and early aughts, Choo used to drink at Von on the Bowery, where he met Cervantes Ramirez, Joseph Schwartz, and Sasha Petraske. When Petraske asked Choo to help him open a new place, he agreed, but only if he could find the perfect location for it. He spent almost three years looking, but finally found the spot he wanted in Chinatown, a neighborhood known more for cheap dim sum than sophisticated cocktail bars. It was a strange space, with no frontage on the street, and a mezzanine constructed by the previous occupants. The landlord and locals who knew the space well told Choo it used to be a wonton factory, but had a secret cinderblock room in the basement where the owners would sell knockoff designer bags. Rumor has it the space was also used as an illegal massage parlor and gambling den. When Choo got hold of it, it had been vacant for five years.

Choo and his partners try to keep things chill by seating everyone, so they'll get the best service and be able to hear each other over the music. This is not the type of place where you'll have to shout to be heard—rather, it's a tasteful, civilized place for craft cocktails made with precision, headed up by co-owner Cervantes Ramirez.

The Ship has never advertised, but gets people coming in who've heard about it by word of mouth. When it first opened, it was so well hidden people searching for it ended up at the bar across the street. Though the door now has the bar's name and logo in gold leaf, it's still one of the more secret cocktail bars. The owners would like to keep it that way.

MULBERRY PROJECT

149 Mulberry Street, New York, NY 10013
• 646-448-4536
• www.mulberryproject.com
• Open daily 6 pm – 4 am
• Transport: B, D trains/Grand St
• Moderate

Bespoke cocktails and street art

If you're familiar with Mulberry Street, you know that it's a surprising location for a secret bar. Located at the crossroads of Chinatown and Little Italy, the street feels oddly frozen in time, surrounded by red sauce joints that have been around since the early 1900s, some of which have served as mafia hangouts. Just a block away, the shop signs are written in Chinese, and pigs and poultry hang on hooks in the windows of restaurants. The area doesn't get much foot traffic from your average New Yorkers. Most of the people on the streets are tourists or Asians who have lived here for generations.

Amid all the bright lights and neon signs of the old-school Italian joints, you have to be looking pretty hard for the unmarked red door with a little red light that serves as the entrance to the Mulberry Project. Step inside and the small, low-ceilinged space is a study in contrasts. With black-leather booths, polished stainless-steel tables and murals by street artists, it feels a bit like a punk rock bar, but without the dirty, divey vibe you'd expect from such a place. Guests hang out at the tables or perch on red metal stools at the bar. A big red mouth reminiscent of the Rolling Stones logo is painted around the little window to the kitchen, where chefs place food orders.

Among connoisseurs of hidden bars, the Mulberry Project is known for its bespoke cocktails. For $15, patrons can choose a spirit, add seasonal ingredients, and decide if they want it shaken or stirred, refreshing or boozy. They serve the classics—Moscow Mule, Bees Knees, Clover Club—as well as daily specials, which tend to be more adventurous. A Channel Orange, made with gin, sloe gin, amaretto, lemon, orange, and egg white, is a semi-sweet, refreshing cocktail served up in a coupe. Other cocktails include jalapeño or Thai chile. Compared with the sophisticated drinks, the food seems lowbrow—tacos, nachos, flatbreads, wings, and burgers might seem better paired with beer. But the high-low combination seems to work.

In the warmer months, the backyard, hidden behind the bar, is open. The small, walled-in space features more murals by street artists like the Brooklyn-based duo Faile. A collage at the entrance is composed of pasted-on photos of Kate Moss and other celebrities. Each summer it takes on a different aspect.

APRÈS-SKI FONDUE CHALET AT CAFÉ SELECT

212 Lafayette Street, New York, NY 10012
- www.cafeselectnyc.com
- 212-925-9322
- info@cafeselectnyc.com
- Open daily from 8 am; weekends 9 am
- Transport: 6 train/Spring St
- Moderate

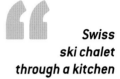

Swiss ski chalet through a kitchen

There isn't a moment in Café Select that isn't impeccably thought through, from the Rolex train station clock (one of three in the world) to the spray paint letters in the bathroom that tell employees to wash their hands. This holistic, almost narrative, design concept extends to what would normally be considered an unusable space–a boiler room behind the kitchen. Owner Serge Becker, the man behind New York institutions like The Box and La Esquina, chose to make it a hidden restaurant from the very beginning when Café Select opened in 2008.

The Après-Ski Fondue Chalet is exactly what it sounds like–a hidden ski chalet accessed through the kitchen of Café Select, if you dare to walk through the door that says "No Entry, Employees Only." Open the door at the back of the kitchen and be suddenly transported to the Swiss Alps. Fondue (in numerous variations) is on the menu, along with everything else that's available in the café out front. You can even get hot mulled wine here, made in a small pot atop a portable burner, just like the lunchtime refreshment popular on European ski outings. This version is mulled with orange, pomegranate, and five different spices: nutmeg, cloves, black pepper, cinnamon, and star anise.

If the front room at Café Select wears its curation on its sleeve, the back room is decidedly loose and unpretentious. There are skis, boots and poles, sleds, and snowboards hanging around the room and nestled in corners. There's an old-school feel, with narrow skis (none of those parabolic ones), colored Christmas lights, and vintage ski posters. A small staircase leads up to a wooden balcony with decorative balustrades, like those found on a Swiss chalet. The corner bar, replete with a few stools, is just a metal slab and the liquor shelves are made of simple wooden boards.

The small space lends itself to coziness, but not towards loudness like so many New York City establishments. The aim is simple here: good bistro food and a cool vibe. This means that Café Select swings towards particular types of clientele—models and fashionistas on one end of the spectrum, and hip everyday regulars on the other—but predominantly New Yorkers. True to the restaurant's mission, the staff is friendly and unpretentious, moving between the two worlds with ease and spirit.

And the best part—in summer, the chalet turns into an oyster shack. "It's Montauk instead of Montblanc," says manager Benoit Cornet. The ski paraphernalia is replaced by fish nets, bikinis, buoys, and lifesavers. It even has a different name for the summer months: Cervantes' Oyster Shack and Bar.

LA ESQUINA

114 Kenmare Street, New York, NY 10012
- 646-613-7100
- www.esquinanyc.com
- Open daily 6 pm – 2 am
- Transport: 6 train/Spring St
- Moderate

Chic Mexican brasserie under a taco shop

The name of this place ("the corner" in Spanish) would have you think it's just your average little corner taqueria. From the outside, it looks very casual, like an old Mexican diner with corrugated tin siding and a neon sign. It's not a front, per se. You could certainly come here and just get some tacos to go. But then you might get curious about where the people disappearing through the door inside the narrow taqueria are going.

If you have a reservation or are lucky enough to get in without one, the host will open the door for you and you'll walk downstairs, through the kitchen (where the Latino chefs are assembling taquitos and ceviche), and into the main brasserie. Behind the long bar, bottles of tequila and mezcal stand at attention. Upstairs, everything is bright, but here it's dimly lit, though not too dark to see the very sensual painting of an odalisque lounging above the sofas. Past a row of iron bars, the dining room feels a bit like a dungeon, but with better food. The tables and chairs are made from a dark wood, and blue-and-white tiles form playful mosaics on the walls. Candles poised around the room are dripping in wax. A thumping soundtrack of pop music sets a party mood.

La Esquina is known for its margaritas and they deliver. Espolón reposado tequila, triple sec, fresh lime juice, and passion fruit or blood-orange juice comes blended together in a goblet with a salted rim and slices of lime and orange. There are other cocktails, including one with vodka, one with gin, and one with bourbon, but most feature tequila or mezcal as the base, and rightfully so. They're the perfect complement to the Mexican street food on the menu. There's the classic *elotes callejeros* (grilled corn on the cob smothered in mayonnaise, *cotija* cheese, and lime juice), ceviche, and *queso fundido* (melted chihuahua cheese with pumpkin seeds and chile de arbol) that arrives in a small cast-iron pan with plantain chips for dipping. And of course, there are tacos in all varieties: grilled steak, chicken, fish of the day, cheese, veal tongue, carnitas, and slow-roasted pulled pork. Each order comes with two tacos, which arrive on a wooden platter. The more you order, the larger the platter that comes out. At around $5 per taco, the price is the only clue that you're definitely not in Mexico City here.

2ND FLOOR ON CLINTON

67 Clinton Street, New York, NY 10002
- 212-529-6900
- www.2ndflooronclinton.com
- Open Tuesday to Saturday 7 pm – 2 am
- Transport: J, Z, F and M trains/Delancey St or Essex St
- Moderate

Through a door labeled "Private"

There's always something fun about having to go through one establishment in order to find the hidden spot inside. 2nd Floor on Clinton is accessed through the back of the restaurant Barramundi on Clinton Street in the Lower East Side through a door labeled "Private" and up a staircase. You'll suddenly feel like you're in someone's country home: on a landing in the staircase there's a little wooden table with a lamp, candle and chalkboard. On a winter visit, it announced that the spiced apricot mulled wine was back. There's a window in the staircase, just like you're outside somewhere, looking into someone's house.

This upstairs location used to be the event space for Barramundi, but owner Tony Powe wanted a place where Lower East Siders could go for cocktails and conversation. Ektoras Binikos, the head mixologist at Michaels's New York, crafted the cocktail menu at 2nd Floor on Clinton, which opened in 2010. There are small bites on the "Nosh" menu like "The Big Dog" hot dog served on brioche and "Fluffernutter & Banana Panini" of crunchy peanut butter, fluff and banana, dusted with powdered sugar. The food is made from ingredients they try (as best as possible) to source from the Lower East Side and New York State. Wine, beer, and spirits are also available.

The decor is an eclectic mix of old-fashioned living room furniture. The mismatched chairs and couches are nonetheless unique, both as items themselves and within the range of New York City speakeasy bar decor. The paper lanterns have real candles inside, red velvet sofas abut the windows, and vintage glass oil lamps sit on the windowsills. A built-in bookshelf is filled with travel books.

Prohibition Night is every Tuesday, with live music and '20s-era cocktails. 2nd Floor on Clinton is also home to the original "Absolut Lowline Cocktail." Urban enthusiasts will be familiar with The Lowline project, a vision to turn an abandoned trolley station nearby into the world's first underground park. In 2013, the Lowline team partnered with local Lower East Side businesses to offer the cocktail, with $1 from each drink donated to the project. The cocktail, created by Binikos, is made with Absolut Vodka, velvet falernum, beet juice, verjus, lemon, gum arabic, aromatic and decanter bitters.

2nd Floor on Clinton is deliberately table service only, so there's no lingering at the bar, and groups cannot be larger than six.

THE BACK ROOM

102 Norfolk Street, New York, NY 10002
- 212-228-5098
- www.backroomnyc.com
- Open Sunday and Monday 7:30 pm – 2 am; Tuesday to Thursday 7:30 pm – 3 am; Friday and Saturday 7:30 pm – 4 am
- Live jazz on Monday nights
- Transport: F, J, M and Z trains/Essex St or Delancey St
- Moderate

Meyer Lansky and Lucky Luciano's Prohibition speakeasy

Imagine this: your guide turns the corner, leading you off busy Rivington Street, where the bars have neon signs, and onto a quiet side street. You almost reach the end when she opens a small metal gate with the words "Lower East Side Toy Company" in block letters, and leads you downstairs to a dark, dingy alley. There's no one else around. Just when you start to wonder if she's going to knife you, she leads you up another set of stairs, where a bouncer asks for a password, and opens a door onto another era. There are gold-framed paintings on red damask wallpaper, a mahogany bar backed by mirrors, antique cut-glass chandeliers, Victorian velvet sofas, and marble coffee tables. People are drinking cocktails in teacups and beers in paper bags. Jazz wafts through the air and the room buzzes with energy.

This is not just another period recreation: this was Meyer Lansky's spot. He and Lucky Luciano (two of New York's most notorious Prohibition-era gangsters) used to come here to conduct "business meetings" with the likes of Bugsy Siegel and Frank "the prime minister" Costello. When the current owners, Johnny Barounis and Steven Yee, started working on the space, they discovered a trapdoor in the restaurant upstairs. During Prohibition, gangsters and bootleggers would drop down into the basement, which had escape routes onto Norfolk, Suffolk, and Delancey Streets, in case the cops showed up.

"Back then, the booze was stronger, so they mashed up fruit, added syrups, anything to mask the flavor of the grain alcohol. Whoever had the sweetest drinks had the best cocktail menu," Yee explains. Today, The Back Room serves classics like the French 75 and the Sazerac in teacups—a throwback to those days when revelers tried to conceal their hooch.

The space has operated continuously as a bar since its speakeasy days, but that doesn't mean it always looked so breathtaking. When Barounis and Yee came in, they spent about eight months restoring the bar to its original beauty. They tore down the wallboard to expose the brick underneath, uncovered the wood floors, built it up again, and found antiques to decorate it. "We wanted it to be a speakeasy," Yee says, "but there's more to that than just a hidden entrance. The difference is always going to be how you run your house." That means they won't tolerate any crap from troublemakers. The entrances are guarded, just like they were in Lansky's day, and only a lucky few will ever make it into The Back Room's hidden back room. Even if you find the bookcase on hinges, that doesn't mean you'll make it past the threshold.

The Back Room is nice any night, but on Monday nights, live jazz animates the space. The band starts playing at 9:00 pm, and people start swing dancing around 10:00.

BEAUTY & ESSEX

146 Essex Street, New York, NY 10002
- 212-614-0146
- www.beautyandessex.com
- Open daily 5 pm – 1 am; Saturday and Sunday brunch 11:30 am – 3 pm
- Transport: F, J, M and Z trains/Delancey St or Essex St
- Moderate to expensive

Swanky nightclub behind a pawn shop

Make no mistake: Beauty & Essex is not for everyone. You don't have to be Jay-Z or Madonna to get in (though they have been known to party here), but show up underdressed and you won't make it past the pawn shop that serves as a front for the luxe nightclub. The retro, mint-green shop up front is clearly a gimmick, but at least it's a fun one. Managing partner Jared Boles says this place has "the keyhole effect," and it's true—it seems small from the outside, but as you continue to work your way in, it gets bigger and bigger, and more and more luxurious.

For over a century, this building had been M. Katz, a furniture store down the street from Essex Street Market, and seeing the club's vast rooms with soaring ceilings, you can almost imagine what that might have been like. When the principals of the Tao Group (the power players behind twenty restaurants, bars, and clubs in New York and Las Vegas) got their hands on the 10,000 square foot space, they completely gutted it and rebuilt from the ground up. Now the place oozes a very theatrical kind of luxury, giving off a retro glam vibe, like the kind of restaurant where Don Draper and Roger Sterling would bring out-of-town clients who wanted to misbehave.

The group took vintage jewelry as their inspiration, spreading the motif throughout the four dining rooms and lounges. An antique brooch inspired an oversized gold floral wall piece on the ground floor. Upstairs, interlocking antiqued mirrors have the shape of one of the partner's mother's bracelet. The Locket Room (the upstairs dining room) features gilded frames that display lockets instead of paintings. (The staff like to put funny photos and images in them—open them up and you'll see.) A pearl chandelier anchors the Pearl Lounge, where the DJ spins and people dance until the wee hours. But the pièce de resistance is the long crystal chandelier that hangs above the grand staircase.

The jewelry theme extends to the menu as well, where drinks have names like the Emerald Gimlet (muddled basil with vodka, lime, and simple syrup) and Earl the Pearl. There's an extensive list of multiethnic share plates, including a whole section of "jewels on toast," like avocado with lemon and espelette on brioche. Star Chef Chris Santos of the Stanton Social is behind the menu, and took every opportunity to play with witty puns and flavor combinations, like the tuna poke wonton tacos—two-bite crispy wonton shells shaped like tacos wrapped around tuna tartar topped with micro cilantro, radish, and wasabi kewpie. The execution of the food is better than you might expect from a nightclub that probably generates much of its revenue from bottle service.

As you'd expect from the name, the place is full of beautiful people—models, actresses, and women that simply look like models and actresses, plus of course the moguls (one patron reportedly racked up a whopping $45,000 tab and left a $15,000 tip). If the ladies take a long time freshening up, it's because the ladies' lounge downstairs gives away complimentary pink champagne—not that they need it.

FIG. 19

131½ Chrystie Street, New York, NY 10002
- info@figurenineteen.com
- www.figurenineteen.com
- Tuesday to Saturday 8 pm – 4 am; Sunday 6 pm – 2 am
- Transport: B and D trains/Grand St; J and Z trains/Bowery
- Moderate

*Behind
an art gallery*

To get to Fig. 19—short for Figure 19 (as if an illustration from a science book)—you have to walk through The Lodge Gallery above the popular subterranean dance spot Home Sweet Home and open up the door in the very back. Once you're inside, it feels like home. In fact, Fig. 19 was created by the owners of Home Sweet Home as a clubhouse for them and the staff to hang out. Originally just an unfinished storage room, they thought, "This could be something better." Home Sweet Home has been a Lower East Side fixture since 2006 and Fig. 19 opened in 2011, a refined update to the woodsy, taxidermy decor of the bar below. First it was just for friends and family, utilizing a membership card system, but now it's open to anyone who knows how to find it.

Everything inside is decorated with the warmth and coziness of a New York City apartment parlor, with the building's original wood plank floor and exposed brick wall. The vintage wooden bar, replete with custom-made animal vertebrae taps, is surrounded by simple stools, while scented candles are scattered throughout the space. Tufted couches built into the wall abut a fireplace fitted with candles and topped with a stuffed peacock. Long, beaded chandeliers hang from the ceiling, including one above a reclaimed wooden table in the back—a great, cozy spot for groups. Friends of the owners curate the art that rotates through the space and a large custom cabinet at the entrance showcases obscura like stuffed birds, skulls, and animal hoof candles. There's also an impressive female bust made of wax whose "tears" were formed when the staff decided to burn the candle.

If you happen to look up, you'll notice that industrial pipes are still exposed and the ceiling is unfinished. Such is the nature of Fig. 19, which has managed to keep away the sceney crowds of New York City by remaining chill and true to its roots. The music that spins in the bar is urban Americana, reminiscent of the sounds that emerged from the indie music scene in Brooklyn in the early 2000s, with references to earlier bands from the '80s like Depeche Mode.

The artisanal cocktails made at Fig. 19 are a tasteful riff on classic cocktails, changing just slightly with the season. The menu was created by the bartender at the Hotel Delmano in Williamsburg, with fun names like Rose Sélavy and Midnight in Paris. There's prosecco on tap (in addition to beers) and a long list of spirits.

There's usually a bouncer in front of the gallery, but don't worry. Say you're headed to Fig. 19, wave to those working in The Lodge Gallery and make your way to the back door.

KUMA INN

13 Ludlow Street, 2nd Floor, New York, NY 10002
- 212-353-8866
- www.kumainn.com
- Open seven days a week 6 pm – 2 am
- Transport: J, Z, M and F trains/Essex St or Delancey St
- Moderate

*Savory,
BYOB Thai joint*

At 113 Ludlow Street on the Lower East Side, there *is* a sign for the Kuma Inn, painted in red on the doorframe in the style of POST NO BILLS, but the boarded-up tenement style building and graffitied storefront look so abandoned, it's impossible to imagine that there's a cozy restaurant upstairs.

For the adventurous, you'd have to first get past the six warning posters in the first floor entrance. Half are from the New York City Police Department, the other half are from Menahata, the Bulgarian bar that occupies the first floor, cautioning in block letters against theft and banning drinks beyond their coat check.

But the Kuma Inn is BYOB, so you just need to banter with the bouncers for Menahata and head up a rickety set of stairs that are barely lit. Pass a closed door on the mezzanine landing and keep going up. You'll see a warm glow ahead emanating from the door and immediately know you're in the right place.

There's a subtlety to the Kuma Inn, both in terms of the decor and the cuisine, that takes time to reveal itself. There are no windows because they're boarded up with plywood. The continuous wall of bamboo ornaments have a lithe, island feel but are functional too, doubling as light sconces. Another art piece consists of multiple compartments, each embedded with different types of rice—a nod to the ingredients of the restaurant. In contrast, the chairs and tables are no-fuss, almost like being in a food stall in a night market in Asia. The main attraction is the narrow, open kitchen where chef and founder King Phojanakong and two cooks are working.

Phojanakong is a New York native, born to a Filipino father and Thai mother. He was trained in the French culinary tradition and is a veteran of the kitchens of David Bouley, Daniel Boulud and Jean-Georges Vongerichten. The name Kuma Inn is derived from the word "*kumain*," or "to eat," in Filipino. The menu is made up of small dishes, which Phojanakong refers to as tapas. Nothing on the menu is over $15, and when the restaurant opened in 2003, there wasn't a dish over $10.

But small dishes do not mean less complexity—in fact, perhaps more so. Phojanakong packs a mighty tradition of flavors and spices into the tapas. Some ingredients, like the sauces and the sausage, are imported directly from Thailand. And anybody who has spent time in Thailand will recognize the exact consistency and flavor of the sticky rice.

The menu is annotated with the signature dishes of the Kuma Inn, like the pan-roasted ocean scallops cooked with bacon, *kalamansi* and sake, the sautéed Chinese sausage, and the yellowfin tuna tartare. The corkage fee ranges from $1 for beer, $3 for sake to $5 for wine. And like night markets, the establishment is cash only.

In a Lower East Side that is rapidly gentrifying, the gritty storefront and simple complexity of the Kuma Inn provide a refreshing, unpretentious alternative.

NITECAP

120 Rivington Street, New York, NY 10002
• 212-466-3361
• www.nitecapnyc.com
• Open Sunday to Wednesday 6 pm – 2 am; Thursday to Saturday
6 pm – 4 am
• Transport: F, J, M and Z trains/Essex St or Delancey St.
• Moderate

*Retro
basement bar*

Nitecap may be one of the Lower East
Side's newest hidden bars, but the
building's boozy history predates the
little watering hole by over one hundred years.
Schapiro's Wine Company was founded in 1899, when the area was full of
Jewish immigrants living in tenements. The family originally pressed the grapes
for their kosher wines in the cellar and sold their wares in the ground floor
storefront. Though the company moved to New Jersey in 2000 and shuttered
in 2007, the buzzy restaurant and cocktail bar that now stands on that block
of Rivington Street adopted the name Schapiro's as an homage to the original.

Down in the old wine store's cellar, Nitecap has taken up residence. Part of
the space was completely empty and unused. When co-owners Dave Kaplan
and Alex Day went inside to renovate, they left the exposed brick as is—stains
and all. They added retro black leather banquettes, a back bar that glows,
tree-patterned wallpaper that changes with the seasons, a little disco ball,
and owl motifs hidden all around. "We wanted the space to feel like your cool
grandmother's basement," says Natasha David, Nitecap's head bartender and
one of the founding partners. Small vintage lamps and fresh flowers make the
space feel homey and a bit nostalgic. Colorful tin cups hanging on the back bar
are used for crushed ice drinks. A playlist full of throwbacks from Nirvana to
the Beatles animates the place.

Call this place a fun neighborhood bar or a sophisticated cocktail bar—
the menu spans both extremes, with $4 beers and $14 cocktails. Kaplan and
Day are known for experimentation, and Nitecap's menu is no exception.
Though rooted in the classics, all of the drinks here are original. The staff's
wit is on display in the menu, which for fall was made to look like a miniature
newspaper dubbed *The Daily Hoot*. "Coming up with the menu is a very
creative, collaborative process," says David, who continues, "Drinking should
be fun. I don't want people to see all the work that goes into the cocktails."
The super smooth Point Blank, for example, seamlessly blends strawberry,
Dorothy Parker gin distilled in Brooklyn, Cocchi Rosa, amontillado sherry,
cinnamon bark, and lemon juice.

True to its name, the bar is a haven for the neighborhood's bartenders, who
come here for the last drink of the night. The place opens at 6 pm and tends
to get busy around 8 pm most days. On Friday and Saturday nights, it gets
so packed there's a line out the door. But for loyal customers they'll hold a
standing reservation at the same time every week. "That feels like the greatest
compliment," David says, and confides that she has regulars who've been
coming to the various bars she's worked at for ten years.

and enter through the unmarked door to the left of the sushi counter in Village Yokocho restaurant. If there's a bit of a wait, be patient. The cocktails here are worth waiting for.

If the rules make you think this place is stuffy, think again. They were instated by the Japanese-born owner, who prefers to go unnamed. He came here to study, but missed the quiet bars back home, where people can actually hear each other talk. When he couldn't find any, he decided to open one of his own. That was over twenty years ago, and Angel's Share has remained one of the more obscure speakeasies to this day. The lack of a website and a dearth of press has kept the bar shrouded in mystery.

Unlike Village Yokocho, which conforms to the typical Japanese restaurant model, Angel's Share feels a bit like your grandparents' salon circa 1965. Heavy, brocade curtains with tassels frame the windows, cut-crystal tumblers sit atop the bar, and two-toned diamond patterned wood behind the bar gives the place a retro look. The pièce de résistance is the hand-painted mural—a copy of Michelangelo's cherubs on the left and right, and a little angel with

BLIND BARBER

339 East 10th Street, New York, NY 10009
- 212-228-2123
- www.blindbarber.com
- Backroom open Monday to Saturday 6 pm – 4 am, Barbershop 12 pm – 9 pm, (Sundays to 6 pm)
- Transport: L train/1st Av
- Moderate

A barbershop in operation that conceals a dance hotspot

Alphabet City was the first location of Blind Barber, which opened in 2010 and has since expanded to Williamsburg and Los Angeles. Reinventing a popular dance spot in the same location, the entrance to Blind Barber is a two-seat barbershop that is actually in operation. Designed to feel like a retro dentist office, even the barber tools are on rolling dental trays. The entrance to the back-room bar is hidden behind a rolling door, which opens up to a large lounge. The name of the bar is a reference to the names given to speakeasies during Prohibition like Blind Tiger and Blind Pig, a message to policemen to turn a blind eye to the activities going on behind the scenes.

In actuality, the style of the Blind Barber back room is a little more quirky than the term "Prohibition" encompasses, designed by Emporium Designs with some personal touches from the owners. One was obsessed with including an abacus, so there's one built into an overhang above the dance floor. Each owner put framed photographs of their grandparents on the walls, but most have been stolen by inebriated customers by now. There's an eclectic mix of tables ranging from vintage chests to shabby-chic finds, even ones converted from barrels. Don't miss the library parlor room in the back past the bathrooms—it's a cozy escape the owners refer to as "Grandpa's Den."

The cocktail menu has a core selection of house classics, like "Strawberry Fields" with vodka, lemon juice, honey, strawberries and parsley, and the "Smoke + Dagger" of whiskey, jalapeño-infused Combier, lemon juice, cucumber, and ginger. The seasonal cocktails change in fall and spring, and pizza is provided until ten at night by Gnocco next door. Happy hours run from a generous 6 pm to 9 pm every day the back bar is open. Evenings get busy—expect the dance floor to be packed.

Back to the barber shop, the small room takes advantage of the original exposed brick of the building. Added to the decor are distressed metal boards, vintage Koker barbershop chairs, and wooden auditorium seats. An old barber-shop sterilizer now functions as a side table. The underlying concept is about camaraderie, a nod to the barbershops of yore where a community would come together. To that end, Blind Barber offers a drink with your shave—anything from spirits to beer. Just no cocktails until the bar opens at 6 pm.

BOHEMIAN

57 Great Jones Street, New York, NY 10012
• By referral only
• www.playearth.jp
• Transport: N and R trains/8th St – NYU; B, D, F and M trains/
Broadway – Lafayette
• Expensive

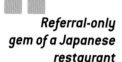

Referral-only gem of a Japanese restaurant

Bohemian is as exclusive and secretive as it gets in New York City—a bar and restaurant that can only be experienced by referral from a previous guest. As the sister bar to the original Bohemian located behind a house in Tokyo, the New York iteration is tucked down a long hallway next to Japanese Premium Beef, a butcher shop on Great Jones Street. At night, the glass storefront gets covered with graffiti-laden metal panels, making Bohemian even easier to miss. Regardless, you won't mosey up to the frosted-glass door of this gem of a Japanese restaurant without knowing someone who has been before. The phone number is guarded jealously. The website is in Japanese with just a mysterious map showing all of Bohemian's locations around the world and information about its work in disaster relief after the Fukushima earthquake.

The restaurant actually leases the storefront to the butcher shop and sources its meats from there. The building itself has a storied history: the carriage house served as the headquarters and saloon for gangster Paul Kelly, was later owned by Andy Warhol, and was the last home of artist Jean-Michel Basquiat, who died upstairs.

Clues to the mission of Bohemian are embedded in the ink-brush map that's on the website, which is reproduced in the bathroom and on the main wall of the restaurant. Besides the existing locations in Tokyo, New York, and Bali, the owner plans to expand Bohemian to even more locations like Hawaii and Germany, making "membership" into this exclusive dining club a global affair. The map shows a spot in Jamaica, too: it's a property for rent, and the property manager curated a recording of Jamaican artists that's framed in the bathroom.

The dining room has a soothing, modern Japanese aesthetic, almost apartment-like with plush low-slung couches and chairs. A rock garden built into the restaurant forms a nice contrast to the modern bar. Art is woven in on many levels: beautiful photography adorns the walls while the plates are designed by different Japanese artists. The backlit bar emphasizes the geometric display case of the alcohol bottles.

The cuisine is a blend of Japanese, French, and American with creative and aesthetic plating. The tasting menu is $58, an experience that should only be tried with an empty stomach. The first course is an impressive farm-fresh vegetable fondue displayed like a flower arrangement. The mushroom-cream *uni-croque* and the Washu beef short-rib sashimi round out the starters. The main course is a pan-roasted *branzino* filled with roasted seasonal vegetables, followed by a choice of Washu beef mini burger or a sashimi rice bowl. The dessert is a delectable yuzu panna cotta. Small plates à la carte are also available with offerings like mac and cheese, foie gras soba, and an ice bucket of fresh oysters.

Despite the long list of whiskeys, spirits, shochu, beers, and wines, the cocktails are on par with some of the best from New York City's speakeasy scene. The libations are a blend of classic New York drinks that mix in Asian ingredients like yuzu, shiso-leaf, and matcha powder.

Simply put, Bohemian serves as a beautiful respite from the sometimes overwhelming scene of hidden bars and restaurants in New York City. The reservation may be difficult to come by, but the experience is anything but pretentious.

PRESS BUTTON & AWAIT FURTHER INSTRUCTIONS

DEAD DROP

166 1st Avenue, New York, NY 10009
• 212-777-1552
• www.deaddropnyc.com
• Open Tuesday to Thursday 6 pm – 1 am; Friday and Saturday
6 pm – 2 am
• Transport: L train/1st Av
• Moderate

Spycraft-themed basement bar

On a generic block along 1st Avenue in the East Village you might notice a sign that says "Dead Drop" with an arrow that seems to point to nowhere. One of the more recent and distinctive hidden bars to pop up in the East Village, Dead Drop puts a clever twist on the genre with its spycraft theme. Instead of craft cocktails, there are "tradecraft" cocktails, and indeed you have to be rather spy-like to come across this bar that came onto the scene quietly.

To access the bar, you have to walk into North River first, then head down the staircase. Press a doorbell, and await further instructions (or just open the door). The red-tinged basement space has the dark red overtones of Cold War espionage and a simultaneously mysterious yet cozy industrial vibe. Water is served in tin cups and the tables are chests made from the aluminum of airplanes. Old telephones and cameras are tucked into corners, a Morse Code tap hangs nonchalantly next to the bar, and Edison light bulbs are everywhere.

Heading to the bathroom is a real trip, down a hallway with exposed pipes and ceramic tiles. Industrial mesh is the material of choice, covering mirrors as well as bottles of vintage booze. The inside of the bathroom has shelves of old books, telephones and a tangle of wires around a non-functioning light bulb. Every table feels like an intimate nook and it's easy to hear the people you're with (without hearing neighboring conversations, appropriately).

The cocktail menu is arranged in espionage-themed categories like "Yet to be Classified," with non-traditional ingredients and "Recently Declassified," which are new creations with classic foundations. Some of the cocktails have truly inventive flavors, like the Khao Yai Park Swizzle, a gin drink with flavors of lemongrass and coconut curry. Drinks have fun names like "Following Orders," "Field Agent," "Fictitious Entry," and "False Flag." The cocktails were devised by Colby Zito, who comes from the culinary side of things, formerly from Eleven Madison Park and Maialino. His strategy is both systematic and creative, taking successful classics and breaking them down into their essential elements, testing "what can be substituted for that ingredient to make something balanced but a little different," he says.

There's a little bit of food too, like an all-black burger and fries with sea urchin mayonnaise. As a last bit of fun, the bill comes embedded in a real book.

DEATH & COMPANY

433 East 6th Street, New York, NY 10009
- 212-388-0882
- www.deathandcompany.com
- Open Sunday to Thursday 6 pm – 1 am; Friday to Saturday 6 pm – 2 am
- Transport: F train/2nd Av
- Moderate

Cutting-edge cocktails in a dimly lit den

There are few places in this city where booze is more loved (and consumed). At Death & Company, a small seating-room-only cocktail bar hidden in plain sight on a quiet street in the East Village, over 200 bottles line the back bar, lit from behind as if spotlighted on a stage. Besides the backlit bar and some candles on the tables, the place is almost pitch black. Sitting in one of the low booths, you feel completely enveloped by the darkness, as if the outside world is a distant memory. But before you can get inside, you have to give your name and party size to the bouncer at the door. If there's a wait for a table, he'll take your number. There's almost always a wait—sometimes an hour or more.

You might be wondering: Why on earth would anyone wait over an hour just for a drink? Because at Death & Co, it's not just a drink—it's an experience, and it starts the moment you approach the door. Once inside and seated at a table, a server will bring you a glass of water and the menu—more of a book, really, with a minimum of fifty cocktails listed at any given time. When you finally decide what to order, you can expect to wait longer than you normally would. Be patient. Death & Co.'s cocktails typically have four to five ingredients, including fresh-squeezed juices, rare amaros, spirits, cordials, and aperitifs. Each drink is prepared with a particular method (stirred with a long metal spoon, shaken in a Boston shaker, strained with a Hawthorne strainer), and served in a specific type of glass. All the recipes have been vetted by the owners and the bartenders, who are certifiable cocktail geeks, so you know they're going to be good.

The duo behind Death & Company, Dave Kaplan and Alex Day, quickly earned a reputation as among the best in the business—a fact they credit to their excellent team. Some of the best bartenders in New York have worked here, and several have gone on to manage other elite bars. "Our best bartenders have dizzyingly brilliant minds. They could be doing anything," Kaplan says. "They're here because they really want to be here." Whenever they get a new bottle, they research its history and origins, what it's typically combined with, and how it reacts to being manipulated.

The whole venture was a bit of an experiment. After working in the service industry for much of his life, and managing a bar in Las Vegas, Kaplan came to New York City knowing only what he *didn't* want to do. Death & Co. was a reaction against the flashy, over-the-top bars of Vegas: it's intimate, dark, and earnest with an emphasis on fresh, handcrafted cocktails. Inside, there are no windows or clocks. "If we're doing our job right," Kaplan says, "you lose track of time."

DECIBEL

240 East 9th Street, New York, NY 10003
- 212-979-2733
- www.sakebardecibel.com
- Open Monday to Saturday 6 pm – 3 am; Sunday 6 pm – 1 am
- Transport: 6 train/Astor Pl
- Inexpensive

Grungy underground sake bar

This little sake bar is not the kind of place that people wander into during a night of barhopping, but it has a dedicated cult following. First you have to find the entrance, with a small sign and a little dormer roof poised above a dubious-looking staircase that leads down into the basement bar. Then you have to make it past the Japanese bouncer guarding an actual rope hung across the waiting room. "Are you meeting friends?" he'll ask, making you wonder if you were supposed to make a reservation. But no, they don't take reservations. They just need to know how many people you're with, so they can find a table for you. There's no standing room, so unless you arrive very early or late, you'll probably have to wait.

Once you get past the rope, you'll cross a short corridor and enter a dark room with a small bar, a couple of booths, a handful of tables, and decorations like a Maneki Neko (the ubiquitous lucky cat). A couple of large Japanese paper lanterns give off a warm glow, casting light on the walls, which are completely scrawled over with graffiti-style messages from past patrons. Though owned by Bon Yagi (the owner of Sakagura), this place feels completely different—like a debauched underground drinking den down a dark alleyway in Tokyo. It's a favorite among the owners of some fancy cocktail bars in the neighborhood.

The bar stocks almost a hundred kinds of sake, with a huge range in price and quality, some served warm, others chilled. There's Japanese beer (Sapporo, Asahi, etc.), plum wine, *shochu* (a distilled spirit with a slightly sweet, nutty flavor), and rare Japanese whiskeys like Yamazaki, which are becoming more popular with bartenders and whiskey aficionados. They serve traditional Japanese bar food too, like sashimi, shumai, okonomiyaki, udon, and soba, which pair nicely with the booze and will help you avoid getting sloppy. By the time you wander back onto the street, you might be surprised to find yourself in the East Village instead of Tokyo.

NUBLU

62 Avenue C, New York, NY 10009
- 347-529-5923
- www.nublu.net
- Transport: F train/2nd Av
- Moderate

> *Nonconformist music haven and club that sometimes offers secret shows*

During the day, the outside of Nublu looks like a shuttered storefront, with metal grates perpetually down except for where the slats have broken off. Sometime between 2013 and 2014, street art appeared which added a splash of color to this otherwise discreet spot in Alphabet City. At night, the only sign of something happening is the little blue light marking the entrance. Inside however, activity is truly buzzing, as Nublu has become a stronghold for musical improvisation across genres. Colin Kasprowicz, a New York-based DJ and musician who regularly performs at Nublu, describes it as "Alphabet City's underground, nonconformist forward-thinking music Mecca."

Nublu had humble beginnings in 2002 as a simple clubhouse where friends of owner Ilhan Ersahin would come and play music. Ersahin, himself a musician on keyboard and the saxophone, describes its early days as more of a rehearsal space. He acquired the wine and beer license just so they could drink during and between jams, as the space was always open to the public. It's a haven for musicians getting their careers started, as well as for famous ones like Moby, Norah Jones and David Byrne, who come to perform secret shows or take in the latest sounds. Moby has said that he "had more fun DJ'ing records for seventy-five people at Nublu than going on tour and performing for 10,000 people a night." Celebrities like Kevin Spacey can sometimes be seen at the bar—it's one of those places you go to for music and inspiration, a place where everyone can do exactly what they feel like. Next to the casual drinkers at the bar may be someone solo dancing up a storm, but it all works.

More than just a club, Nublu is also a record label, which launched in 2005. It's hard to define the music exactly, as the Nublu label is more about curating taste with its roots in beatnik. There's the rhythmic dance music of Brazilian group Forro in the Dark, the jazzy trip-hop of early group Wax Poetic (who had early Norah Jones as a vocalist), the experimental Nublu Orchestra, along with electronica artists from the New York area and abroad. Most recently launched is the Nublu Jazz Festival in New York City, Rio de Janeiro and Istanbul.

At the bar, expect a wide range of sake, along with beers and wine. Nublu will eventually move down the street, below Studio 151, a fairly hidden recording studio and bar also run by Ersahin. The old space will stay in Ersahin's hands but might be something totally unexpected, as is to be expected from Ersahin, with a sushi place being considered.

PLEASE DON'T TELL

113 St. Mark's Place, New York, NY 10009
- 212- 614-0386
- www.pdtnyc.com
- Open daily
- Transport: L train/1st Ave; F train/2nd Av
- Moderate

Through a vintage phone booth

Please Don't Tell (or PDT as insiders know it) is one of the more memorable speakeasy-style experiences, mainly because you enter it through a vintage phone booth in a hot-dog shop. For first-time visitors, this is quite astonishing. Coming in off the street, you walk four steps down into Crif Dogs, a divey little hot-dog place with a fast-food style counter, a few tables, and arcade games. Just to the left is a vintage phone booth. Slide the door open, pick up the receiver of the red rotary phone, and dial 1. A hostess will answer and grant or deny you entry by opening a door on the other side. The process is certainly reminiscent of a speakeasy—if you have an "in" (a reservation will do) you'll be admitted, but if not, you might be told to wait.

Inside, the contrast between the shoebox-sized bar and Crif Dogs couldn't be greater—a fact the bar has capitalized on. PDT is dimly lit and done up in the style of a 19th-century tavern, with a low ceiling fashioned from diagonal wooden slats, a few black leather booths, a long copper bar, and taxidermy-adorned brick walls. If you sit at the bar, you'll be packed in tight, but you'll have the best vantage point to see what the bartenders are mixing up. Jim Meehan, the bar's co-founder and partner behind the cocktail program, is a self-declared cocktail geek. He wrote the *PDT Cocktail Book*, edits *Food & Wine* magazine's annual cocktail book, and is the Drinks Editor of *Tasting Table*. Under his guidance, PDT won the James Beard Foundation's inaugural Outstanding Bar Program award in 2012. Though he no longer lives in New York City, his influence can still be felt.

At any given time, the menu features a list of eighteen cocktails. Every few months, a couple are switched out and others are introduced, tied loosely to the seasonality of the ingredients. Bottles are lined up in front of the mirrored backbar, and glasses, tools, bitters, and garnishes are kept within easy reach, so bartenders won't be slowed down looking for things. There's a certain theatricality to the way they stir and shake drinks—sometimes several at a time—which can only come from mastering the techniques. Dressed up in suits and ties, they certainly look the part. The bar serves hot dogs from Crif Dogs, including some special recipes by high profile chefs David Chang, Wylie Dufresne, and Daniel Humm.

PDT has garnered a lot of press in New York City and around the world, so it caters to a large tourist population, especially on weekends. Weeknights are calmer and see more locals and industry people coming in to talk shop.

What most people don't know is the bar's creation story. Co-owner Brian Shebairo opened Crif Dogs first and got a liquor license before the East Village's community board made them more and more difficult to get. When he and Jim Meehan opened PDT in 2007, they avoided applying for a new liquor license by putting the bar on the same property as Crif Dogs, without a separate street entrance. Thus this speakeasy was born.

THE RED ROOM

85 East 4th Street, New York, NY 10003
- 212-787-0155
- www.redroomnyc.com
- Open Friday and Saturday 9:30 pm – 2:30 am and for private events
- Transport: F train/2nd Av
- Moderate

Jazz Age speakeasy above KGB

There's nothing secret about KGB Bar, the Soviet-inspired literary outpost in the East Village. Writers—both esteemed and unknown—have been doing readings there for over twenty years. But The Red Room above KGB, which traces its roots back to Prohibition, is another story.

Outside on the street, a neon sign announces KGB, but there's no indication of the Red Room. The building on East 4th Street that houses both bars, as well as the Kraine Theater, was built in 1858 and briefly housed the Women's Aid Society. In the '50s and '60s, the Ukrainian Labor Home, a social club for Ukrainian socialists, occupied the building. They hosted banquets on the first floor and operated their own private speakeasy on the second floor. But before the Ukrainian Labor Home bought the building in 1948, notorious gangster Lucky Luciano ran a speakeasy called the Palm Court there.

Today, The Red Room on the third floor operates as an event space and speakeasy of sorts. Though most people climb the narrow marble stairs only up to the second floor, if you keep going up, you'll find an unmarked red door with a gold Art Deco peephole. Cross the threshold and you'll find yourself in an intimate bar where the decor and cocktails are throwbacks to the 1920s. Owner Dennis Woychuk, a native New Yorker, restored the tin ceiling and brought in period decor, like the Art Deco wall sconces from a Detroit movie theater. He has been involved with the building since 1983, when he operated an art gallery in what is now the Kraine Theater. As a kid, he used to come to the Ukrainian Labor Hall with his father. He had his first taste of whiskey there at the tender age of five.

While KGB hosts literary readings, The Red Room hosts 1920s belly-dancing shows, live jazz, and private events. At the front of the room, a small red-curtained stage is set up for intimate performances. The music is enough to transport you to a timeless New York, where strangers become friends over a round of drinks and time inches on toward the wee hours of the morning. Settle in with a Gin Rickey—F. Scott Fitzgerald's favorite—a French 75, or a champagne cocktail with Angostura bitters. One too many and you might end up in the big copper tub at the end of the night.

RUSSIAN AND TURKISH BATHS CAFÉ

268 East 10th Street, New York, NY 10009
- 212-674-9250
- www.russianturkishbaths.com
- Open 365 days a year
- Transport: L train/1st Av; 6 train/Astor Pl; N and R trains/8th St — NYU
- Inexpensive

An East Village institution

There may be no greater social equalizer than the Russian and Turkish Baths in the East Village. In an earlier era, lower Manhattan was dotted with bathhouses where residents from all walks of life would come to steam, cleanse, and revitalize. One of today's last bastions is on 10th Street between 1st Avenue and Avenue A, staying strong and distinctive amidst a rapidly changing neighborhood.

Opened in 1892, the baths have welcomed not only the local community but also celebrities like Mick Jagger, Frank Sinatra, and John F. Kennedy Jr. As reported by the *New York Times*, legend has it that the Russian "Radiant Room," a veritable inferno of 15 tons of rock cooked overnight, was built from the headstones of cemeteries.

The restaurant at the baths is completely hidden from the street, with nary a window in sight. Stepping inside is not unlike being transported into a Cold War shelter that wasn't notified in 1989. A VCR feeds into two televisions while old newspaper clippings about the spa line the walls. A single worker behind a long deli-like counter serves up classics like Russian borscht soup, Polish sausage, Siberian *pelmeni*, and Baltic herring. Bringing the place incongruously into the 21st century are the American breakfast omelets and smoothie bar, with offerings like Energy Booster and Fantasy Island.

Wine and beer are also available, but if the managers take a liking to you, they just might give you a taste of their own stash of cognac and other spirits. Plastic and styrofoam cups are brought out, food is shared, and a family is born. On your way out, they'll give you hugs and kisses.

The latest owners of the Russian and Turkish Baths are Boris Tuberman and David Schapiro, who bought the baths together in 1985 but operate on different weeks due to a dispute between them going back to 1993. Visiting on a "Boris week" is a completely different experience from visiting on a "David week," both in terms of amenities and clientele. David has opened the baths to Groupon deals while Boris has not; multi-visit passes sold by one owner are not honored by the other. The quirky backstory is told in hot steam rooms by long-time patrons who say they have to keep their calendar organized in order to remember which weeks they can take in the baths.

As you leave, refreshed enough to take on the city that never sleeps, revel in the kitschy wall murals of the Greek and Roman baths and sit on the park bench that is placed in the entranceway of the East Village tenement building. In a few seconds, you'll walk outside down a set of stairs and re-enter the present day, leaving a small, disappearing pocket of New York City.

STREECHA UKRAINIAN KITCHEN

33 East 7th Street, New York, NY 10003
- 212-674-1615
- Open Friday to Sunday 11 am – 4 pm
- Transport: 6 train/Astor Pl
- Inexpensive

Homemade food by church volunteers

Streecha Ukrainian Kitchen is one of those spots that doesn't have to try—either to be known or to be hidden. It's accessed through the basement door of an East Village brownstone that houses a chiropractor's office, located diagonally across from St. George Ukrainian Catholic Church, with which it is affiliated. When it first opened, the only thing that denoted its existence was a piece of laminated paper hanging from a clothes line, with the names of three dishes. Over time, one paper sign became two sheets on the window. Today, there are two vinyl signs, one completely in Ukrainian and the other with the restaurant name on it. Still, it remains nondescript and very easy to miss on a block that has other high-profile destinations like McSorley's Ale House, one of the oldest bars in the city.

Restaurant is a misnomer however, as it has the feel of a church canteen, which it is. But it's open to the public, with operating hours on Friday through Sunday. The menu is small but targeted, offering four main dishes: borscht soup (in cup or bowl), Ukrainian potato dumplings known as *varenyky*, stuffed cabbage with pork and rice called *holobutsi*, and sausage with sauerkraut. The dumplings are hand-rolled starting as early as six in the morning by church volunteers. The proceeds from the kitchen support the church and its private school.

The parish of St. George has been in the neighborhood for over a hundred years and Streecha Ukrainian Kitchen is straight out of the 1970s, when it first opened. The walls are of beige tile and sky blue paint. The tables are covered with polyester tablecloths and the metal folding chairs clang around as visitors rearrange the seats along the long communal tables. Condiments like salt, pepper, mustard, and sugar are displayed in Tupperware boxes, and religious paintings hang on the walls to complete the picture. Despite the dated atmosphere and fluorescent lights, the place buzzes with positive energy during popular hours, just like a get-together at a community organization.

The fare is simple and affordable with the dumplings at $0.75 a piece, the hearty stuffed cabbage at $4.00, and the cup of borscht soup at just $2.00. The coffee is nothing to write home about, but it's just $1.00. There's also an assortment of baked goods like powdered jelly donuts, cinnamon danish, and cheesecake, along with packed Hostess Donettes.

The hours can be unpredictable—the food's available until it runs out, basically—so get here on the earlier side of the afternoon and bring cash.

WILLIAM BARNACLE TAVERN AT 80 ST. MARKS

80 St. Marks Place, New York, NY 10003
- 212-388-0388
- Open Monday to Friday 6 pm – 2 am; Saturday and Sunday 1 pm – 2 am
- Transport: 6 train/Astor Pl; L train/1st Av

Prohibition-era mafia escape routes

Though the William Barnacle Tavern itself is no longer hidden, the bar is one of the few authentic speakeasies left over from Prohibition, and the building itself still holds a rich history of secrets—including intact mafia escape tunnels and safes.

In 1964, bar owner Lorcan Otway's father was a struggling actor looking for a theater. When a man named Walter Scheib offered up a former speakeasy for very cheap, it seemed like a no-brainer. During the renovation, Lorcan and his father came across two unopened safes. Otway's connection with the entertainment industry gave him the insight to suspect, as the business was closely tied to mobsters then. To touch their belongings was risky, perhaps deadly. They got in touch with Scheib and opened the safes together. One was nearly empty but the other contained two million dollars. Otway kept the bar (and his life) but Scheib took the money.

But Scheib wasn't the real owner of the money—it was Frank Hoffman, a Bavarian gangster who was also Scheib's partner in the Prohibition era. Hoffman had placed around $12 million in the safes, which was enough money to buy the entire Lower East Side back then. It appears that Hoffman and his girlfriend left in a hurry taking what they could carry. Lorcan suspects that they were killed by Hoffman's driver who likely knew about the money.

Downstairs from the bar are remnants of the escape tunnels used by Hoffman, now a storage room that you can see on visits to the Museum of the American Gangster, a two-room museum connected to the theater run by Lorcan. A vintage wooden telephone, used to alert gangsters of upcoming raids, still hangs on the wall next to a barred window. On the window itself, Otway's father found copper wire, which he surmised used to be connected to a bomb. It's not surprising given that Scheib once packed the wall of the upstairs bar with explosives to protect against police raids.

The entrance to the bar was originally through a butcher shop next door, concealed from the street. Behind the bar was a dance hall, which became a jazz club later and is now the theater. The horseshoe-shaped bar is only half the size it was during Prohibition. Half of it was stolen—Lorcan's father often loaned half out as a stage set. Today, an enormous mirror, actually an optical glass for a screen projection, gives visitors a sense of what the bar would have looked like in its original form.

The William Barnacle Tavern specializes in absinthe—twenty-eight kinds in fact—and single malt scotches. Lorcan used to be a shipbuilder, so the maritime theme of the bar is a nod to his past, creating a divey, "non self-conscious" pub. Unlike many of the trendier Prohibition-style bars in New

York City, the tavern is not only authentic, every item in the bar also has a fascinating history connected to Lorcan and his family. Lorcan himself is often behind the bar, making 1920s-inspired cocktails or serving absinthe. Ask him the story of the theater and he'll happily bring you back in time.

Follow the yellow street art-style rabbit painted onto the external wall of this Greenwich Village beer bar and go down the rabbit hole. Except for that rabbit, the exterior of this place is completely black and nondescript. But head downstairs and into a tiny, cave-like bar for one of the best beer selections in the city.

> *Beer bar with a '60s rock'n'roll vibe*

You might feel like you've stepped into a dingy 1970s watering hole, with rock'n'roll posters taped up on the brick walls, especially if they happen to be playing the Rolling Stones. Though much of Greenwich Village—especially Macdougal Street—has become a victim of its own hipness, the Old Rabbit Club feels like a stalwart reminder of the Village's bohemian roots. Nearby you can still see the bars like Cafe Wha? where Bob Dylan and Jimi Hendrix performed for beatniks and hippies in the '60s, though now they mostly cater to NYU frat boys and tourists. Perhaps because of its secrecy, the Old Rabbit Club feels much more authentic. The only unfortunate relic of times past: it's

THE GARRET

296 Bleecker Street, 2nd Floor, New York, NY 10014
- 212-675-6157
- www.garretnyc.com
- Open seven days a week
- Transport: 1 train/Christopher St
- Moderate

Chill spot above Five Guys

The Garret is one of those bars where the bartenders are like your bandmates or your awesome guy roommates. Hidden above Five Guys burgers in Greenwich Village, you have to walk to the very back of the fast-food joint and up a wooden staircase. From the outside, you can only spot some chandeliers through the window and a neon sign that says "Soul," simply because the bar has soul, claims one of the bartenders. The actual sign of The Garret sits on the bar itself.

It's the type of spot where you can start day drinking at 2 pm on Saturdays, order a can of Tecate and a shot, and bring up burgers and fries from downstairs. But there are also the impressive creative cocktails with names like "Seriously Ain't Fancy" and "Sunken Santa." It has a laid-back cool that you'd find in a dive bar anywhere around the country, with just the right amount of curation in the decor to have personality without pretension. With street art under the fireplace, hilarious photographs, old books and hourglasses scattered around, it manages to please both the trendy cocktail connoisseur and those looking for an easy spot to chill.

The inside of the bathroom door is lined floor to ceiling with ninety-six gold doorknobs in an almost surrealist work of art, installed by Greenwich Locksmiths. Greenwich Village residents will recognize the nearby locksmith shop, with its façade made entirely of swirling locks.

The wooden chairs and tables could have been pulled straight out of a treehouse, fitting because the space is blessed with two enormous skylights, making it a rare hidden bar with tons of natural light.

For those still looking for exclusive gems, there are Five Guys burgers you can order that aren't available at any other location, like The Garret Burger using Peter Luger sauce, the Italian Neighbors burger with Ottomanelli Bros prosciutto, and the Sixth Man Burger with sriracha.

But most importantly, you'll leave The Garret feeling like you found a bar that feels genuine: both a great place to bring friends or to stop by and chat with the gregarious bartenders. With so many exclusive places in New York City on the cocktail circuit, The Garret is a breath of fresh air.

LITTLE BRANCH

20 7th Avenue South, New York, NY 10011
- 212-929-4360
- No website
- Open daily 7 pm – 3 am
- Transport: 1 train/Houston St
- Moderate

A
family affair
in a basement bar

On a bustling block of 7th Avenue, around the corner from the swimming pool with the mural that Keith Haring painted, stands a little flatiron building with a nondescript brown door. On busy nights, there might be a bouncer waiting, but if there isn't, you can get close enough to see a peephole, the likes of which are on many an apartment door in this city. The subtle message seems to be: come drink in my house, but act respectfully, as if you were my guest.

Once in the door, you'll have to descend a long staircase into the basement bar. It's easy to imagine that this is what a true speakeasy would have looked like—not some opulent temple to booze, but somebody's humble basement where hooch was shared with friends the owner knew he could trust. There is certainly a '20s vibe emanating from the place. Look around and you'll notice the pressed tin on the bar, the slightly beat-up brown leather booths, the tables made from safety glass, the corrugated tin ceiling, the vintage cash register with keys like a typewriter's, and the black-and-white family photos and knick-knacks (including many period pieces from that era).

Little Branch is the second bar opened by Sasha Petraske and Joseph Schwartz, who have a hand in several of New York's most renowned cocktail bars, most notably Milk & Honey. And like many Prohibition-era speaks, this is largely a family operation. Joseph manages the bar, his younger brother Ben is the head bartender; and bartender Becky McFalls is married to Joseph's twin brother Louis, who waits on tables. Down in the basement bar, they serve classic cocktails as they were intended to be served, according to precise recipes laid out in books like *The Savoy Cocktail Book*, published in 1930 by Harry Craddock, an American who went to London to escape Prohibition and became a renowned barman at the American Bar at The Savoy.

Little Branch was among the first bars to always make cocktails with fresh juices and stock the liquors that they like best, regardless of how expensive or hard-to-get they are. There's a small menu printed with a list of classic cocktails, but you'd be just as well off going with the bartender's choice. They pride themselves on listening to what you like and making something that fits the bill. The beginning of the week is the best time to come, as wait times are shorter, and there's live jazz starting at 10 pm.

LATE-NIGHT RAMEN AT TAKASHI

456 Hudson Street, New York, NY 10011
- ramen@takashinyc.com
- www.takashinyc.com/
- Friday and Saturday midnight – 2 am
- Transport: 1 train/Christopher St or Sheridan Sq
- $16+

> *Foie gras ramen after hours*

By day, Takashi is a Korean barbecue joint in the West Village, serving up all things beef. In the restaurant's own description, "Our menu is beef, all beef, and nothing but beef!" After hours, behind closed doors and by reservation only, Chef Takashi Inoue offers his take on the ramen craze hitting the city. Upon arrival, a lantern on the ground emanates a warm glow to mark the entrance. You'll see the thirty-four-seat restaurant packed beyond a "Sorry We're Closed" sign.

While ramen is traditionally made from chicken, pork or fish broth, Chef Inoue takes what he knows best—beef—and makes a decadently rich, beef-broth ramen. The broth is made over the course of 24 hours by simmering beef bones with garlic, ginger, and herbs.

The late-night menu offers only one dish, ramen, in two different varieties: Takashi's Original Ramen and Grandma's Spicy Ramen. Both come with U.S. Kobe braised-beef belly, crispy small intestines, Japanese seaweed, and organic soft-boiled egg. You can get extras of any of the ingredients, even Grandma's Spicy Paste, or for the adventurous, a "Foie Gras Sensation" topping for an additional $14.

Inoue was born in Japan to third-generation Korean immigrants, and his cuisine is a blend of both cultures. Each of the toppings in the late-night ramen has a story, like the crispy small intestines, which are a delicacy in Chef Inoue's hometown of Osaka, Japan. Grandma's Spicy Paste is inspired by a recipe from Inoue's grandmother, who owns a *yakiniku* restaurant in Osaka. The ramen noodles are made fresh, from a traditional technique known to result in a smooth texture. The beef comes from high-end purveyors like Pat LaFrieda and Dickson's Farmstand in Chelsea Market.

The late-night seatings for ramen only started in early 2014, but the space seems made for after hours. The interior of Takashi is warm and inviting, with reclaimed wood chairs and tables. You can also sit at a counter in front of the open kitchen to watch what's being prepared. By night, the light from the restaurant spills out onto the otherwise quiet West Village street.

A whimsical painting stretches around the entire right wall of the restaurant, painted by a friend of Inoue. It's an informative mural, covering the history of the dishes on the menu and answering questions about the health of the dishes, like "Do you think meat is fattening?" (Answer: "That's a misunderstanding.") and "What's *horumon*?" (A part of the cow usually considered "discarded goods" that Inoue is particularly dedicated to).

There's also an extensive sake and wine list, which includes Japanese plum wines. If you're unsure, the very friendly staff are happy to give you a tasting first. Finally, the staff are what really sets Takashi apart, even after hours. They seem just as passionate about the food as Chef Inoue is, curious about how you heard of the restaurant, and eager to tell you more about it.

VIRGOLA

28 Greenwich Avenue, New York, NY 10011
• www.virgolanyc.com
• Open Monday to Sunday 2 pm – midnight
• Transport: A, B, C, D, E, F and M trains/West 4th St; 1, 2, 3, L, F and M trains/14th Street
• Moderate

> **Wine and oysters in an 1800s alley**

T hough in a well-trafficked neighborhood, and not as hidden as some of the other bars around, Virgola is a special case. This bar is in no ordinary building: it's tucked into an alleyway from the 1800s, which was uncovered and carefully restored. When owner Joseph Marazzo was building this Italian wine bar, he wanted to replicate the way thresholds in Rome feel under one's feet, as if the stone from outside continues inside. Luckily for him, the unusual space that houses Virgola has bluestone floors common to Greenwich Village.

The outdoor-indoor barrier is certainly tenuous here. A tall wrought-iron gate guards the entrance. Brick walls painted black recall a dark alley. When Marazzo was renovating the space in 2013, an old woman approached to see what he was doing. She told him that she had played soccer in the alley as a girl, bouncing a ball off the brick walls with her friends. Later, she said, she snuck in with a neighborhood boy and had her first kiss here. Upon hearing this story, Marazzo knew that he wanted his bar to feel romantic, the kind of place lovers might steal away to be alone. With the woman's help, he was able to replicate the original gate, adding details like the Vs. When he opened Virgola in August 2013, he gave away a hundred love locks, which guests inscribed and hung on the gate, the wall sconces, and the wrought-iron table legs, following the tradition of the love locks on Ponte Milvio in Rome.

Marazzo is third-generation Sicilian, and Rome holds a special place in his heart. His girlfriend at the time was Roman, and while she was arguing with him one day, she shouted "*virgola*," the way Americans might enunciate "period" at the end of a sentence for emphasis. Marazzo didn't immediate know what "*virgola*" meant, but deduced that it was the Italian word for "comma"—a pause that indicates a shift in a sentence. He named his bar Virgola: a place to take a break.

Guests certainly feel like they've been transported to another place. The tiny alley, just 6 feet wide, is too narrow for a bar. Instead, guests mingle in crimson leather booths or at one of the black wooden tables. They sip wines carefully chosen by Marazzo (all Italian) or cocktails. You'll find classics like a Negroni, or try one of Marazzo's concoctions, like the Virgola, with gin, *cocchi* Americano, squid ink, tomato water, sea salt, and pepper. The best deal? The oysters, farmed from Montauk, Duxbury, MA, and Prince Edward Island, and always $1, no matter the hour.

EMPLOYEES ONLY

510 Hudson Street, New York, NY 10014
- 212-242-3021
- www.employeesonlynyc.com
- Open daily 6 pm – 4 am
- Palm reading and tarot cards from 7 pm on
- Transport: 1 train/Christopher St
- Moderate

> **Art Deco speakeasy behind a psychic sign**

If you've ever strolled through the West Village, you've probably noticed the proliferation of psychic shops, though it's rare to see people going in and out of them. If it weren't for the perpetual lines, it would be easy to bypass the door on Hudson Street near Christopher Street with the neon psychic sign in the window. But those who do might never know that hidden inside is an award-winning cocktail bar and restaurant. Push aside the red velvet curtain in the vestibule, where an actual psychic reads palms and tarot cards from 7 pm on, and you'll find yourself in a gorgeous bar.

The details are all Art Deco here. Wall panels are curved mahogany, a three-tiered ceiling molding draws the eye upward, where pendant lamps hang. The backbar's inch-thick glass shelves glow greenish along the edges, and the liquor bottles lined up are illuminated from behind. Opposite the curved brass bar, a few tables are positioned along the wall, where reproductions of '20s- and '30s-era paintings and photographs by artists like Man Ray, Tamara de Lempicka, and Juan Gris hang with museum-style lights above them. There are vintage suitcases poised on a shelf over a beveled mirror, and a small metal fan in the corner. Before Employees Only opened in 2004, this space was Caffe Sha Sha. Back in the 1920s, it was a funeral parlor, and the marble floors are from that period. The fireplace, now framed by thick shiny metal, dates back to the building's original construction in the 1860s.

Behind the bar, bartenders elegantly dressed in white shake complex cocktails. There are classics, EO takes on the classics, and originals, like the Mata Hari, a blend of Remy Martin 1783 Cognac shaken with chai-infused Martini Rosso and pomegranate juice. After a bout of vigorous shaking, the bartender pours the concoction through a Hawthorne strainer into a coupe, and garnishes it with rosebuds. The drink is subtly sweet, smooth, and delightful. Many of the cocktail recipes change seasonally, so the Ginger Smash, made with fresh cranberries in winter, might be served with pineapple in summer.

In the back room, elevated by a few steps, guests dine on oysters, steak tartare (hailed as the best in the city), bacon-wrapped lamb chops, and ricotta gnocchi. In the back, there's a bit more space to get comfortable, with pale yellow banquettes and tables. On a shelf positioned high on the wall, the owners' collection of vintage shakers, mixers, and seltzer bottles holds court. After midnight, the kitchen switches over to a late-night menu, which features the kind of dishes you might crave after a long night of drinking—truffled grilled cheese with parmesan fries, chicken schnitzel, and Balkan street sausage, among them. The kitchen stays open until 3 am, and at 3:30 am they play Tom Waits and serve a free cup of chicken soup to the last brave souls in the bar—often service industry professionals who come for a nightcap after their shift. "When we opened, there wasn't a place where you could finish your shift and come for a good cocktail, a good meal, and have fun. We tried to tie it all up," says co-founder Igor Hadzismajlovic.

BATHTUB GIN

132 9th Avenue, New York, NY 10011
- 646-559-1671
- www.bathtubginnyc.com/
- Open seven days 6 pm – 2 am; until 4 am Thursday, Friday and Saturday
- Transport: A, C and E trains/14th St
- Moderate to expensive

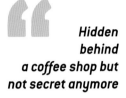

Hidden behind a coffee shop but not secret anymore

Like Beauty & Essex in the Lower East Side, Bathtub Gin is a hidden bar in Chelsea that has capitalized on the speakeasy trend in New York City, run by a large restaurant group that knows how to hit all the right elements. You don't necessarily go to either of these places for the most authentic experience, but they are spots in the hidden bar vein that make things easy for larger groups. At Bathtub Gin, there's food, a big drink list, bottle service, live entertainment, and space. And it's well hidden.

Bathtub Gin is located behind a concealed door inside Stone Street Coffee Company, a roaster from Brooklyn with a tiny outpost on 9th Avenue. Come 6 pm, the coffee shop is filled mostly with people waiting to get into Bathtub Gin. Reservations can be made on OpenTable and the hostess is set up on the side of the coffee shop checking in guests and taking walk-ins, along with a bouncer who checks IDs.

The inside of Bathtub Gin is large with many different seating arrangements. There's a long bar lined with aperitivos and bitters and there's a row of high tables across from the bar. The main room has banquette seating on the sides with velvet damask couches. Chairs and settees form small groups in the center. The centerpiece of the bar is the copper bathtub with claw feet positioned perfectly for photographs and selfies.

The bathtub in general, a nod towards the days of Prohibition when booze was homemade in bathroom tubs, forms a central design element. You'll find smaller copper bathtubs as sinks in the restroom, another one on the bar functioning as an ice bucket and a tiny one as decoration close to the ceiling. The ceiling is tin, of course, and the floors are unvarnished wood. The damask pattern continues onto the wallpaper, which is adorned with a small collection of Prohibition-era photographs familiar to all, like the "We Want Beer" protesters.

Besides the cocktail list, which is arranged by liquor type, there are cocktails made from Bathtub Gin's proprietary small-batch rum developed in partnership with Mount Gay Rum in Barbados. It comes neat and on the rocks. The food menu ranges from small plates to larger dishes like duck confit or skirt steak. Cured meats and cheese plates round out the menu, plus desserts like chocolate truffles, crème brûlée, and toast your own s'mores. The most expensive item on the menu is the $1,075 bottle of Hennessy XO cognac.

THE LODGE AT GALLOW GREEN

542 West 27th Street, New York, NY 10001
- 212-564-1662
- www.mckittrickhotel.com/#GallowGreen
- Open Monday to Friday 5 pm – late; Saturday and Sunday 4 pm – 1 am
- Transport: C and E trains/23rd St
- Moderate

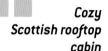

Cozy Scottish rooftop cabin

There are few places in New York City more immersive than the McKittrick Hotel, hidden in plain sight under the High Line in Chelsea. The McKittrick isn't a hotel at all: it's the home of *Sleep No More*, the award-winning interactive play based on Shakespeare's *Macbeth*. Rather than watching the action unfold on stage, at *Sleep No More*, audience members are given matching masks and encouraged to wander through the dark, cavernous building, where scenes from the play unfold simultaneously in many different rooms. *Sleep No More* has had people buzzing since it opened in 2011, but it's far from the only thing to see in the McKittrick.

No one who's attended the show could have seen the whole building—it encompasses 100,000 square feet and a hundred rooms. The whole place is shrouded in mystery. Legend has it the McKittrick was built in 1939 as New York City's most lavish small hotel, favored by Alfred Hitchcock, who named the hotel in *Vertigo* after it. Yet shortly after opening, its fortune soured with the advent of the war. The McKittrick shuttered its doors and no one involved with it was ever heard from again. It's said to have remained abandoned and untouched for over seventy years, until the current owners came in and found all the furniture still intact. This is all uncorroborated, of course, but a visit to the McKittrick is only fun if you suspend your disbelief.

The McKittrick's creators have made it easy to leave the outside world behind and immerse yourself in the mystery and lore. Besides *Sleep No More*, there are several ways to experience it for yourself. There are dinners at the Heath, late-night musical performances at the Manderley Bar, and—the most special of all—the rooftop bar, Gallow Green. In spring and summer, the rooftop feels like an enchanted garden in Provence circa 1940. Arches covered in wisteria line the path from the door to the bar and seating area. An antique train car sits empty, tattered lace curtains billowing in the breeze. People gather at vintage tables and wooden benches, sipping McKittrick mules.

In the winter, Gallow Green is transformed into The Lodge. The warm, cozy space is modeled on Scottish bothies—bare-bones cabins up in the hills where people can camp out for free provided they leave something useful behind for the next guest. Completely surrounded by pine trees, The Lodge takes you mind and body out of New York City. Like *Sleep No More*, it's nothing less than a theatrical experience with every single detail thought through, even the layer of dust that sat on the mantel on opening night.

The cabin has a few distinctive seating areas, made up of groupings of worn leather club chairs, cushioned benches, and a rocking chair draped with a blanket in front of the fireplace. Boughs of dried flowers hang from the ceiling and antique wall sconces cast a warm glow while a jazz singer croons. There's a long communal table, bunk beds outfitted with hot-water bottles and plaid blankets, and a separate bedroom with a writer's desk and shelves lined with antique leather-bound books.

Space heaters tucked under bunk beds and inside nightstands add to that cozy, cabin feel. Black and white photos are tacked up on the walls, an antique map of Scotland hangs from the ceiling, and handwritten letters are tucked into the desk's drawers. There is, of course, a bar, tucked into the corner near an old porcelain washbasin. Grab a hot drink, like a steaming mug of mulled wine or a camping cup of rye-spiked cinnamon cider, and settle in. And don't miss the fire on the outdoor patio or the tent filled (and we mean *filled*) with sheepskins in a remote corner of the forest.

NORWOOD

241 West 14th Street, New York, NY
- 212-255-9300
- www.norwoodclub.com
- Open to members Monday to Saturday 10 am – 3 am
- Many events open to non-members
- Transport: A, C, E and L trains/14th St
- Moderate to expensive

> *Lavish arts club in a Chelsea townhouse*

Norwood, a private arts club hidden in a Chelsea townhouse, is not the easiest place to get into, but if you can get an invitation, go. A business lunch in the main floor lounge would be quite nice, but the place really comes alive after dark, when you're apt to feel like Alice in Wonderland peeking behind doors where you probably don't belong. For a non-member, that's the fun of Norwood. It's so luxurious and exclusive that getting a glimpse inside feels like entering some kind of fantasy world.

Built by esteemed merchant Andrew S. Norwood in 1847, the townhouse retains its historic details, including elaborate crown molding, mahogany doors, and marble fireplaces. It is listed on the National Register of Historic Places. Despite its historic pedigree, Norwood is a thoroughly modern club. It has 1,100 members and a flurry of events, which range from members' supper clubs to live performances to art openings. Non-members can rent space as well, for business meetings, parties, and weddings. Members sign the guestbook when they enter, and guests of members check in with the receptionist poised under the stairs in the entrance. Once inside, guests are free to explore. The townhouse occupies six floors and each one seems more over-the-top than the last. The various salons, lounges, and dining rooms were decorated by owner Alan Linn and Simon Costin, a set designer who did stagings for Alexander McQueen's fashion shows and whose work regularly appears in *Vogue*.

Start on the main floor lounge, where a delicate black chandelier made of tree branches hangs above the bar painted with birds in flight. Then, ascend the steps to the dining room, outfitted with plush red velvet banquettes, a bar with an ethereal glass installation hanging above it, and works by Damien Hirst and other artists on the walls. The next floor up is the salon, with an eclectic rock'n'roll vibe. Here, the large bar seems framed on three sides by a tapestry-like banner. Order a Tanqueray and tonic and settle onto one of the inviting couches, under paintings by members and photographs like the one of Andy Warhol and Basquiat. The top floor houses the screening room, a rather simple space, especially compared with all the rest. Downstairs, a hidden door leads down to the basement, where a private dining room with an equestrian theme provides an intimate space for dinners.

Norwood is a home for the curious—a place where artists and those who appreciate the arts can mingle across generations, exchange ideas, and make lasting connections.

RAINES LAW ROOM

48 West 17th Street, New York, NY
- www.raineslawroom.com
- Open Monday to Wednesday 5 pm – 2 am; Thursday to Saturday 5 pm – 3 am, Sunday 8 pm–1 am
- Transport: 1, 2, 3, F and M trains/14th St
- Moderate

> ## Classic cocktails in a Victorian parlor

You can't just open the door and walk into Raines Law Room. Like at the Prohibition-era speakeasies, you have to ring a doorbell and wait to be greeted. A man—looking suspiciously like a butler—will offer to take your coat and lead you through heavy velvet curtains into the parlor, for that's exactly what it appears to be. With sofas made of tufted velour, damask wallpaper, a fireplace, antique mirrors, and vintage pictures framed in gold, the bar looks for all the world like a Victorian salon. The decor certainly facilitates conversations and romantic assignations. Four little nooks along both sides of the room were created by grouping two velour sofas to face each other, with translucent curtains separating them. Each nook can seat up to six guests, ensuring the group's intimacy, with a little service bell to ring when you'd like to order a drink.

Raines Law Room is a civilized place, but that doesn't mean you can't have any fun here. Open your leather-bound menu and you'll immediately see the story of Raines Law, which in 1896 prohibited the sale of alcohol on Sundays, except in hotels. All you needed for a hotel was a couple of shabby rooms to let above a saloon. Raines Law hotels started springing up like wildfire. Far from the intention, these little hotels were breeding grounds for prostitution and other societal ills. This cocktail bar's name is a cheeky nod to Raines Law.

The cocktails sprung out of the Milk & Honey school. Partner and head bartender Meaghan Dorman drank at Milk & Honey, Little Branch, and Death & Company when they first opened. At the time she worked at a restaurant in Harlem, but she was looking for somewhere that felt more like a home. She found Raines Law Room on craigslist and was hired as one of the founding bartenders. "I think cocktails especially then were great for bringing out the geek in people," Dorman says. She used to pore over vintage cocktail books, reading them during her daily commute on the subway. She believes you've got to learn the rules before you can break them.

Michael McIlroy (formerly of Milk & Honey, now at Attaboy) trained the opening staff. All the hallmarks of a great cocktail bar are there: a wide variety of spirits, amaros, and syrups, fresh fruit and herbs and oversized ice cubes that won't dilute the drinks too much. The task of distinguishing Raines Law Room from its predecessors was left largely up to Dorman. She created a menu that grouped drinks together by their characteristics (shaken and refreshing, stirred and strong, a hint of spice, spritzes, and a page of staff picks). She hopes this will encourage people to try spirits they might not be as familiar and comfortable with, whether that means rye, cognac, or pisco. The bar, which you'll reach by walking through the parlor, resembles a kitchen, with a large sink, small refrigerator, and an island for prepping the drinks. Glass cabinets encase rare and expensive liquors as well as delicate antique glasses. Though there are no barstools, people often hang out back here when they want to chat with the bartenders, just as they would hang out with the host in the kitchen during a dinner party. Finally, don't miss the wallpaper design—it's not what it seems from afar.

DEAR IRVING

55 Irving Place, New York, NY
- www.dearirving.com
- Open Monday to Thursday 5 pm - 2 am; Friday to Saturday 5 pm - 3 am; Sunday 5 pm - 1 am
- Transport: 4, 5, 6, L, N, Q and R trains/Union Sq
- Moderate

A time traveler's fantasy

I n his film *Midnight in Paris*, Woody Allen explores the idea that everyone—no matter when they were born—feels a kinship with a certain era in the past. Maybe it's just the romantic notion of being able to look back on a simpler time with rose-colored glasses, which, of course, is impossible except in hindsight.

Dear Irving was inspired by that idea—that anyone can feel aligned with a period in history, and might feel at home if they could immerse themselves in it. The bar, located in a historic townhouse on Irving Place where O. Henry lived, has a time-traveling theme.

Dear Irving comprises four rooms that climb farther and farther into the past: up front is a '60s-inspired room with midcentury modern furniture, zebra-striped wallpaper, and decorations. Next, there's a '20s-style room, fit for Gatsby and Daisy, with oversized silver armchairs and crystal curtains. The next room back houses the actual bar, which continues with the '20s theme until it abruptly becomes an 1880s themed room, all red upholstery and pressed-tin ceilings. The final room is Rococo-themed, like Marie Antoinette's parlor. There are Louis XIV armchairs, white molding with gold trim, an antique mirror, and a huge crystal chandelier. You can find your place and stick to it or wander between the rooms.

Dear Irving is owned and operated by the team behind Raines Law Room and the Raines Law Room at the William, and the cocktail program (presented like a hotel folio) was designed by Meaghan Dorman. You could easily stick to the house drinks, like the Vice Versa (gin, grapefruit, bitter, pamplemousse liqueur, and rosé cava), or go with the bartender's choice.

There's a menu of small plates too, done up in the style of upscale bar food, and inspired by various European traditions: croque monsieur, chicken liver and foie gras parfait, a shrimp cocktail and a cheese plate. A little plate of slow-cooked octopus with almond cream and tomato confit comes out of the kitchen so perfectly (tender yet firm), it'll change your mind about octopus forever, and it will make you think twice about your standard bar-food choices.

There are desserts too, like the sublime panna cotta, which arrives in a cocktail glass, under a layer of red berry coulis with strawberry garnish. This is definitely a place to come when you want to indulge.

TAPROOM AT THE PLAYERS CLUB

16 Gramercy Park South, New York, NY 10003
- 212-475-6116
- www.theplayersnyc.org
- Open to members Monday to Friday 5 pm – 10 pm
- Many events open to non-members
- Transport: N, R and 6 trains/23rd St
- Moderate

> **The oldest private club in New York City still in its original location**

There aren't many places left in New York where you can imbibe whiskey and gin surrounded by artifacts like Mark Twain's pool cue, 19th-century Shakespearean costumes, and portraits by John Singer Sargent. The Players Club, a Greek revival townhouse on Gramercy Park, is one of these places. In fact, it is the oldest private club in New York City still in its original location. Walking into the Players Club feels like stepping back in time to the Gilded Age. Yet because it has always been a private club, few people know about it.

In New York City real-estate terms, the Players Club is enormous—sprawled out over four stories, plus the grill and taproom on the lower level. In the parlor, a large fireplace, antique sofas, tables, and club chairs greet visitors. Upstairs in the card room, guests can see where Mark Twain and Stanford White played poker. The library is full of books and artifacts relating to the theater, including a bust of Edgar Allen Poe and black and white photographs of the actresses who were not allowed to be members (the club was male only until 1989).

Downstairs in the grill and taproom, Mark Twain's pool cue hangs near the pool table. Portraits of the club's famous members (including John Barrymore, Cary Grant, Gregory Peck, Liza Minelli, Ethan Hawke, Kevin Spacey, and Jimmy Fallon) line the walls of the stairwell and the taproom. If you're lucky, you might get a glimpse at the Players Club founder Edwin Booth's bedroom on the third floor. It still smells of the tobacco he smoked incessantly and contains his most cherished objects, including the skull that a fan left to him to use in *Hamlet*.

The club's illustrious history began as a result of one of the most turbulent events in American history. After John Wilkes Booth assassinated President Lincoln, his brother Edwin Booth (a great Shakespearean actor) felt he had to do something to remove the stain on the Booth family name. In 1888, he founded the Players Club, a private club where actors (considered rabble rousers at the time) could meet men of society and elevate their status. Fifteen other incorporators joined him, including Mark Twain and William Tecumseh Sherman. Famed architect Stanford White (a club member) redesigned the façade that looks out over Gramercy Park and the statue of Edwin Booth in Shakespearean garb. Club members can use the key that opens the gates to the private park.

The Players Club is open to members Monday through Friday. The club hosts many events, including readings and interactive plays, giving non-members the chance to see this incredible place.

MILK & HONEY

30 East 23rd Street, New York, NY
• Transport: N, R and 6 trains/23rd St
• Moderate

The speakeasy that started it all

Milk & Honey is probably the most influential speakeasy-style cocktail bar in New York, thanks to its heavy influence on countless bars that came after it. The bar originally opened on Eldridge Street, where Attaboy currently stands. Milk & Honey's first incarnation was so exclusive that cocktail connoisseurs desperate to go had to finagle a way to get the unlisted number and call to make a reservation. For many, it was a sure sign of elitism and a huge turn-off. For others, it was a revelation. In fact, the Milk & Honey school goes far beyond this bar and the others co-owned by Petraske. He and his protégés have trained countless bartenders and proprietors in the old-school way of making classic cocktails.

In the beginning, owner Sasha Petraske thought that by not cooperating with the press, he could keep them away, but it wasn't long before people caught on to the place and discovered it for what it was—a great cocktail bar with bartenders who really care about cocktail culture, mixing drinks for a relaxed but discerning clientele. The moniker is a biblical allusion—in the cocktail desert of Chinatown, the bar was a metaphoric land of milk and honey.

Petraske admits now that some of his initial decisions were not the best way to run a bar. While Milk & Honey was originally reservations only, he realized that such a strict door policy would only perpetuate the snobbism he wanted to avoid. The real reason for the hidden entrance is respect for the neighbors. Growing up in Greenwich Village, above Caliente Cab and a perpetually loud bar, Petraske was well aware that noise complaints could ruin his relationship with the neighborhood and could spell the downfall of the bar. When he opened Milk & Honey, he promised his landlord that the place would be discreet.

You won't see any long lines to get in or people crowding around the bar, trying to get the bartender's attention. There's minimal standing room. Privacy is fundamental to Milk & Honey, and there are printed rules. This is a place where people can sit in a booth and hear each other talk. You might hear jazz in the background, but you won't be bothered by the conversations of the people around you. This may not seem like a big deal, but New Yorkers know that it's a luxury not to have to shout over the noise in a crowded bar. Petraske wanted the overall atmosphere to be like a tenement that received an Art Deco treatment. The steel tabletops are scratched up from people's keys, and family photographs hang on the walls.

There's no written menu (though Petraske might add one at the bar's next incarnation). Order a classic cocktail or the bartender's choice. Trust them—they know hundreds of cocktail recipes, and make drinks with the freshest ingredients available. A daiquiri made with fresh lime juice squeezed in a juice press, sugar syrup, and Bacardi heritage light rum is good enough to make you understand why Hemingway and countless others loved the classic cocktail so much.

Though the bar is temporarily closed, Petraske has confirmed that Milk & Honey, in a new location, will reopen in 2016.

GAONNURI

1250 Broadway, 39th Floor, New York, NY 10011
- 212-971-9045
- www.gaonnurinyc.com
- Open seven days a week for dinner, lunch Monday to Friday
- Transport: B, D, F, M, N, Q and R trains/Herald Sq or 34th St
- Moderate to expensive

Korean atop an office building with amazing view

There is such a density of restaurants in Koreatown on 33rd Street near Herald Square that there has to be a good reason to visit one of the most upscale on the block.

On the 39th floor, the top level of a nondescript office building at 1250 Broadway, Gaonnuri offers an amazing panorama of the city: a 180 degree view of midtown Manhattan—from the Hudson River looking onto Jersey City to Herald Square and Bryant Park, and the MetLife Building atop Grand Central Terminal. In one corner, you'll find yourself nearly face to face with the Empire State Building.

The restaurant is spacious, with two sets of tall horizontal windows wrapping it. The decor is almost theatrical, stepping down into a semi-circular seating area. The tables by the windows are also equipped with barbeque capability, though the design is so sleek you wouldn't necessarily notice it when the grill is covered.

You can tell Gaonnuri thinks pretty highly of itself, starting with the decor and the dress code. "Please dress appropriately," the sign says, with a list of clothing guests should "refrain from wearing," like sports caps, baggy or ripped jeans, tank tops, flip flops or sneakers.

Go during lunch for the best deal. The lunch *bansang* offers *bulgogi* (traditional marinated sliced beef rib-eye) for $20 or *kalbi* (marinated beef short-rib) for $25. Both come on a wooden tray with rice, soup, and individual side dishes, known as *banchan*. The *banchan* are refillable, and in addition to the classics like *kimchi* and spinach, there are some that are not commonly offered at the other Korean restaurants down the street, such as a dish of pickled bellflower with cucumber and squid. The *bulgolgi* bansang comes on a bed of onion and scallion, with a slice of pumpkin.

The barbeque lunch starts at $23 for chicken and $25 for *bulgolgi* and sliced pork belly. Other classics like *mandoo* appetizer (steamed dumplings), *japchae* (stir-fried glass noodles), *galbi tang* (short-rib soup), *kimchi jiggae* (spicy *kimchi* soup with pork and vegetables) and *bibimbap* (rice mixed table side in a hot stone bowl with meat, seafood, or vegetables) are also on the menu. And not surprisingly, as this is both a tourist and business lunch destination, there's an extensive drink menu of hard liquor, wine, and cocktails. Long story short: the food is decent, but the view is better.

THE GARRYOWEN AT THE 69TH REGIMENT ARMORY

68 Lexington Avenue, New York, NY 10024
- www.sixtyninth.net/armory.html
- Open only to military personnel and their guests
- Armory sometimes open for events
- Transport: 6 train/28th St
- Inexpensive

Hidden bar for the military

The 69th Infantry Regiment, known in popular culture as "The Fighting Irish," was initially an all-Irish brigade founded to train Irish immigrants in America to free Ireland from British control. The regiment has had an illustrious history fighting in the Civil War, World War I, World War II and the Iraq war. Wild Bill Donovan, the WWI Medal of Honor awardee, was also part of the 69th and went on to be in charge of the OSS, a forerunner to the CIA. The 69th was also one of the first responders at Ground Zero, going in against orders. Their motto, "Gentle when stroked, fierce when provoked," references the Irish wolfhounds on their coat of arms. There's even a James Cagney movie, "The Fighting Irish," about them.

The regiment's landmarked armory on Lexington Avenue and 25th Street is still active and you can get in when they open for events. In fact, the 1904 building is landmarked because the building hosted the first New York City Armory Show in 1913, not for its military history.

The architects of the armory were Hunt & Hunt, who also designed one of the Vanderbilt mansions on Fifth Avenue. The immense arched drill hall has remnants of wonderful wood auditorium seats on the second floor. There are also historical artifacts from the regiment's involvement in various global conflicts in glass cases throughout the entrance hall and in the main reception room. The wooden doors inside and at the entrance are reinforced and resistant to pistol fire, a remnant of the security needs when the armory was built.

But the real hidden gem inside this armory is The Garryowen, a bar that began as an officers' club but now welcomes military personnel and their guests. The wood-paneled space, named after the regiment's marching tunes, got its current look around 1962, but existed in an earlier form prior to that. A marble fireplace is flanked with massive artillery while personalized beer steins line the walls, flipped upside down for enlistees who are gone. There's also a relic of the World Trade Center framed on the wall. One of the biggest days at The Garryowen is St. Patrick's Day where upwards of 400 to 500 people come by. Despite the rowdiness, we're told only one person has ever been banned from the bar (for life). The offering is simple with beers on tap and standard cocktails. The real experience when visiting The Garryowen is about the stories you'll hear.

MIDDLE BRANCH

154 East 33rd Street, New York, NY 10016
- 212-213-1350
- Open nightly 5 pm – 2 am
- Transport: 6 train/33rd St
- Moderate

*Escape
from Murray Hill*

Like the other bars in Sasha Petraske's network, Middle Branch is a no-fuss destination focusing primarily on offering visitors perfected, fresh cocktails. That's not to say that the decor is without charm—in fact, it feels just like a townhouse you'd like to own. It's a fresh change from the rambunctious, college-age destinations that normally fill this neighborhood. In contrast, this Murray Hill speakeasy is denoted only by a circular crest with the initials MB on the outside, as the windows have been replaced with frosted glass. There's a slightly imposing wrought-iron gate out front, but don't worry. Just head to the entrance, which is on the basement level.

In a space converted from an antique shop, the two-floor bar is connected by a wood and metal staircase. The basement level has tall bar tables and table lamps of a style that would normally decorate a living room. The main floor, which would once have been the parlor room of the apartment, has two floor-to-ceiling windows, also frosted. In the warmer months, the wrought-iron balconies are open for views of the Empire State Building.

Exposed brick surrounds most of the room with a marble fireplace as the centerpiece. A hat, scarf, and sweater hang on hooks in the wall—left behind by guests as if in a real house. The tables are wooden butcher block with cast-iron legs, like you might find in an old tavern. Once again, nothing is over the top here—just elegant.

Although the bartenders have over 500 cocktails they can make off the top of their head, the menu is organized simply. A list of classic cocktails like the Martini, the Old Fashioned, and the Manhattan, is counterbalanced by a changing menu of new cocktails. Freshly squeezed juices are mixed with spirits and syrups for tart and mildly sweet cocktails in lemon and lime. There are sipping spirits including absinthe, amaro, and pisco, beer, wine, and champagnes, and non-alcoholic ginger beer. You can buy bitters, silver straws, and absinthe spoons for your home bar, too. For some unique drinks off the menu, ask for the Queens Park Swizzle, a Trinidadian version of the mojito, or the Don Lockwood, made from bourbon, single malt scotch, maple syrup, and chocolate bitters.

The very last page of the menu has a few quotes about bartending, which hammer home Petraske's convictions about the business: "Bartending is an old and honorable trade...The idea of calling a bartender professor or mixologist is nonsense," from the 1934 forward to *The Official Mixer's Manual* by Patrick Gavin Duffy, the bartender of New York City's Ashland House who served drinks to people like J.P. Morgan, Oscar Wilde, and Mark Twain.

RAINES LAW ROOM AT THE WILLIAM

24 East 39th Street, New York, NY 10016
- www.raineslawroom.com
- Open Monday to Wednesday 5 pm – 1 am; Thursday to Saturday
  5 pm – 2 am
- Transport: 4, 5, 6, 7 and S trains/Grand Central
- Moderate

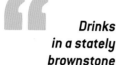

***Drinks
in a stately
brownstone***

The second location of Raines Law Room at The William, a luxury extended-stay hotel for the modern traveler, may be even more befitting its name than the original spot. After all, the famous loophole in the Raines Law of 1896, which prevented the sale of alcohol on Sundays except in hotels, prompted a flurry of saloons to add furnished rooms.

As such, co-owner Yves Jadot chose the location of Raines Law Room deliberately, after a long search. The William is located in the former home of the Williams Club, a private club for the alumni of Williams College in Massachusetts. The two stately interconnected brownstones were an appropriately historical setting for the East Coast liberal arts college, founded in 1793, the same year George Washington was sworn in as the first President of the United States. In 2010, the Williams Club decamped to the Princeton Club's building on West 43rd Street and the townhouses were renovated by Jadot.

Raines Law Room is technically located on the parlor floor but it's accessed through the basement bar, The Shakespeare Pub. From there, the host takes you through a door marked "No Admittance," through velvet curtains and up a staircase. Because of the townhouse layout, Raines Law Room is split into two rooms across from each other. One room contains the bar and a few alcoves of seating, separated by long curtains. For those familiar with the original Raines Law Room, the bar room is probably most reminiscent of their first location. The parlor room across the way is designed like a house library, with backlit bookshelves, wing chairs and tufted couches. Candles illuminate the dark marble fireplace, while suggestive paintings harken back to the brothels of an earlier New York. Also look closely at the wallpaper and what look like floral flourishes are actually bodies of naked women, a design element introduced at the original Raines Law Room. Also like the original location, service bells built into the walls notify the wait staff you're ready to order.

The cocktail menu is similar to the original spot too but with more old-fashioned influence, with head bartender Meaghan Dorman in charge of cocktail development at both. Instead of a menu organized by spirit type, there are three simple categories: Bright & Fresh, Stirred & Strong, and With a Hint of Spice. Then there's the "Choose Your Own Adventure: Old Fashioned" where you pick your bitters, sweeteners, and spirits. You can also order a specially curated menu of small bites from The Peacock restaurant, also inside The William, while at your seats.

This outpost of Raines Law Room at The William is a nice addition to the Murray Hill and Midtown East neighborhoods and a perfect complement to the hotel, but the original location has more of the old-school speakeasy feel. As the menu says, choose your own adventure.

CAMPBELL APARTMENT

15 Vanderbilt Avenue, New York, NY 10017
- 212-953-0409
- www.hospitalityholdings.com
- Open Monday to Thursday 12 pm – 1 am; Friday and Saturday 12 pm – 2 am; Sunday 12 pm – midnight
- Transport: 4, 5, 6 and 7 trains/Grand Central
- Moderate to expensive

*One
of the most
magnificent rooms
in the entire city,
within
Grand Central*

Of all the hidden bars in New York City, the Campbell Apartment is the grandest and most elegant. Yet of the 750,000 people who pass through Grand Central Terminal every day, only a fraction knows it exists. The next time you want to impress someone, lead them to the gilded elevator in the south-west wing of the terminal, below Commodore Vanderbilt's enormous gold light fixtures lined with Edison bulbs, and take them downstairs to the basement. There, up a small set of stairs, you'll find one of the most magnificent rooms in the entire city.

To fully appreciate the Campbell Apartment, you need to know its history. In 1864, industrialization was beginning to dramatically alter the landscape and politics of New York. Cornelius "Commodore" Vanderbilt had risen from humble beginnings to become a shipping magnate and one of the wealthiest men in the country. After making a fortune in steamships, he bought out the railroad and set about rebuilding Grand Central to reflect his wealth and glory. He let his friend, the tycoon John W. Campbell, set up a private office inside the station starting in 1923. At once, Campbell furnished the place with Oriental rugs, 13th-century Italian furniture, priceless porcelain vases, a huge leaded-glass window, and an enormous stone fireplace. Campbell lived in the suburbs, but took great pride in his gorgeous office, and often entertained guests there in the evenings. He used the space until the 1940s.

After Campbell moved out, the room was used as a holding cell for the police, CBS's executive offices, and was left empty and abandoned for a while before it finally reopened to the public as a cocktail bar in 1999. A renovation in 2007 restored the Campbell Apartment to its former glory, making it the epitome of Gilded Age splendor in New York City. You can even see Campbell's original safe, with his name engraved on it, under the fireplace. The cocktail list harkens back to the Jazz Age, with fresh takes on classic drinks, the most celebrated being the Prohibition Punch—a fishbowl-sized serving of passion-fruit juices, Appleton Rum Estate VX, and Gran Gala topped with Moët & Chandon champagne. One is all you'll need to feel like a robber baron on par with the Commodore.

KURUMA ZUSHI

7 East 47th Street, New York, NY 10017
- 212-317-2802
- www.kurumazushi.com
- Open Monday to Saturday 11:30 am – 2 pm; Sunday 5:30 pm – 10 pm
- Transport: B, D, F and M trains/7-50 Sts – Rockefeller Center
- Expensive

Remarkable sashimi flown in from Japan

If you're in the market for truly remarkable sushi, look no further than Kuruma Zushi, run by chef Toshihiro Uezu since 1977 on the second floor of an office building in Midtown. A word of warning: sitting at the sushi bar and agreeing to the chef's choice (*omakase*) can run upwards of $300 per person. If that's within your budget, we guarantee that it is worth every penny, with delicacies like *toro* (fatty tuna), *uni* (sea urchin) and king crab made like art in front of you and delivered piece by piece. The sashimi melts in your mouth, full of rich, sea flavors rarely found in ordinary upscale sushi restaurants in New York City. Even the rice is cooked to a level of perfection and temperature. Some of the fish is flown in from Japan daily—Uezu got his start as an apprentice in a restaurant just near the Tsukiji Fish Market in Tokyo.

The experience at Kuruma Zushi is described by critics and food lovers as "euphoric," "transcendent," and "ethereal" and the experience at the sushi bar is made even more memorable with the presence of Uezu himself, who bellows out welcomes in Japanese and English. Throughout the *omakase*, he'll ask if you want to try other things, like the Russian king crab and it's hard not to resist his enthusiasm and broad smile. He'll also describe the apprenticeship process, notoriously tough in the sushi industry, in front of the latest apprentices. The last one, he says, didn't last too long. Despite the banter, the assistants continue to make sushi with utmost concentration.

The good news for mere mortals is that there's a regular menu too, with lunch at a reasonable $25 for sushi and $30 for sashimi. The tuna lunch specials, three rolls of tuna or a sliced fresh tuna filet over a bed of rice, start at $25. Even with the entry level price point, the quality of the sushi is evident, and the placement of wasabi and garnishes so exact, no extra wasabi is given. There are also classic Japanese appetizers like *sunomono* (fish and seafood marinated in rice vinegar) and *oshinko moriawase* (pickled vegetables).

Decor-wise, the restaurant looks lifted right from Japan. The main attraction is the L-shaped sushi bar, with a smaller sake bar closer to the windows. A large ink-brush painting dominates one wall and an abstract design akin to a Japanese rock garden is behind the sushi bar. You can request seating at tables by the windows or book a private room in advance.

The service is excellent: even the front door opens just at the right moment as you scale the staircase, as there's usually a staff member standing just behind the door. New cups of tea are brought over as you approach the bottom of your current serving and the escalator is called as you sign your bill. And yes, what looks like part of a Japanese temple actually houses the elevator. You'll take the single flight down, sometimes sharing it with people that work upstairs who are unaware of the restaurant, pass by the small security desk and exit back onto the busy Midtown streets.

NORWEGIAN SEAMAN'S CHURCH COFFEE SHOP

317 East 52nd Street, New York, NY 10022
• www.sjomannskirken.no/new-york/
• Tuesday to Sunday, hours vary
• Community gathering place intended for Norwegian expatriates and visitors
• Transport: E and M trains/Lexington Av or 53rd St
• Inexpensive

Norwegian snacks in a church sanctuary

From the outside, the Norwegian Seaman's Church looks like a government consulate, save for a stained-glass window on the façade. Given the other consulates located on this street in East Midtown, it's easy to walk right past it. But ring the buzzer and you'll first see a cabinet filled with coffee cups that come from many different Norwegian ships. It's a little hint of what comes next, behind the doors of the church sanctuary.

The Norwegian Seaman's Church was formed in 1878 to minister to visiting sailors, serving as a home away from home. Over the years, the church has evolved to serve the Norwegian expatriate community in New York City, functioning more like a cultural organization. As such, tread lightly if visiting: they're welcoming, but it's clear this place is intended for Norwegians. Further proof: the website is completely in Norwegian.

The back of the sanctuary is a café, serving tea, coffee and Norwegian waffles, along with soft drinks. Though there is a wooden counter with a cash register, the café selection is displayed on a long church table covered in a tablecloth. The waffle plus tea or coffee combination is $3, with sugar and jam as topping. You serve yourself on a fun platter with a built-in spot for your coffee cup, featuring the monogram of the church. Once a month, they serve a buffet lunch featuring Norwegian delicacies. Adding to the coziness, there's a brick fireplace (non-functional) and a grandfather clock.

One of the best finds here is the small grocery corner filled with Norwegian staples, including chocolates, licorice, baking ingredients, jams, and packaged soups. There's even a waffle maker.

You'll hear predominantly Norwegian spoken here, making it a real escape. The Norwegian Seaman's Church has been in this location for over twenty years. The upstairs floors are apartments for Norwegians sent to the United States for work. Downstairs, the Trygve Lie gallery has regularly changing exhibitions, and on the mezzanine is a reading room. It's a far cry from when Norwegian churches were on floating boats on the Hudson River but there's still a strong sense of community that can be felt here. A similar, more well-known institution, the Swedish Church on East 48th Street, serves up an affordable lunch of open faced sandwiches, with cinnamon buns and lingonberry juice.

SAKAGURA

211 East 43rd Street, New York, NY 10017
- 212-953-7253
- www.sakagura.com
- Lunch Monday to Friday 11:30 am – 2:20 pm; dinner from 6 pm every day
- Transport: 4, 5, 6 and 7 trains/Grand Central
- Moderate

> *Japanese village beneath a Midtown office*

With its entrance far from the street, Sakagura is one of those truly hidden places.

Open since 1996, it's located in the basement of a nondescript Midtown office building. Pass the security desk through a pristine white lobby and go down the stairs. Cross the threshold of the restaurant and you'll suddenly feel as if you've entered a Japanese village.

The decor is such that diners have the impression they're sitting outside, with interior façades that look like houses, replete with windows, shutters and dormer roofs. Wood and bamboo are the main materials of construction, and though the architecture isn't by any means an exercise of purist Japanese form, the raised level of the sake bar area, a mini Shinto shrine and rice paper dividers give it a homey feel in spite of its basement location.

Cuisine-wise, it's one of the finest for Japanese in New York City at affordable prices. It's also one of those Japanese restaurants where you can order inventive non-sushi dishes and revel in delicious hot foods you might ordinarily only get in Japan. For appetizers, try the Washu beef self-cooked on hot stones, a sea urchin soup with soft boiled egg and salmon roe, the *onsen tamago* (a slow-cooked poached egg in cold soup), the *buta no kakuni* (a special stewed diced-pork dish), or the *chawanmushi* egg custard topped with thickened ponzu soup. For the main course, try the miso stewed beef tongue with shitake mushrooms, spinach, taro potato and daikon radish. There are over two hundred types of sake served, including their own exclusive kinds.

The bathrooms at Sakagura are shaped like oversized sake barrels, with interiors decorated like a small apartment. For those that haven't experienced the automatic Japanese toilets, you're in for a treat. The lid will open automatically when you enter, the seats are heated and there are various cleaning and drying options (but you can still do a simple flush).

Upstairs, tucked behind the elevator bank, is a small Japanese bodega, with ready-made take out food from Sakagura. On a visit, don't get confused with the other Japanese restaurant, the Soba Totto Bar, which is right on the street.

Owner Bon Yagi also owns the sake bar Decibel in the East Village, also subterranean, but with a completely different vibe.

UNITED NATIONS DELEGATES DINING ROOM

United Nations Headquarters General Assembly Hall, United Nations
Plaza, New York, NY 10017
- 917-367-3314
- http://visit.un.org
- Open Monday to Friday 11:30 am – 2:30 pm
- Reservations by telephone at least 24 hours in advance
- Transport: 4, 5, 6, 7 and S trains/Grand Central
- $29.99 buffet with UN ID badge, $34.99 without badge

**_Dine
amidst
dignitaries_**

Although the United Nations Headquarters can be visited on guided tours, one of the best-kept secrets is the Delegates Dining Room. Despite what its name suggests, the restaurant is also open to the public with advance reservation.

The dining room reopened in 2014 following extensive renovations to the General Assembly building, the first update since the United Nations complex opened in 1952. The buffet format at the dining room means that you'll be brushing past and sitting amidst ambassadors, dignitaries, and delegates, all while taking in impressive views of the East River, Roosevelt Island, and Long Island City.

You'll have to go through an airport-style security and ID check, but the process is quick. On the way to the dining room, you'll get a chance to walk through the iconic entrance hall of the General Assembly. Due to security requirements you have to be escorted, but the escort functions more like a guide, pointing out fun facts about the buildings. It's almost like having your own exclusive tour.

The entrance to the Delegates Dining Room is like a step back in time to the mid-20th century. Floor to ceiling wooden beams flank the opening where you'll be confronted first by the long buffet spread. Inside, the decor is not particularly impressive, but the views from the nearly floor-to-ceiling windows are. The mod-style chairs seen in vintage photographs of the dining room were replaced long ago by more heavy-handed furniture and the entire space is carpeted like a Mad Men-era office building. There is a wonderful outdoor terrace, but it's used only for special events.

The "internationally inspired" buffet is prepared by an executive chef and changes daily. A rainy-day visit in December showcased a hearty offering. A chef was carving a rack of lamb, there was duck confit, truffle parmesan potatoes, acorn squash, and brussels sprouts with turkey bacon. Four different types of salads were available along with a cold-cut selection that included gravlax, Italian mortadella sausage, and tuna. The dessert table is nearly as long as the entree table and has a variety of tarts, macarons, parfaits, cakes, pies, and fresh fruits. The cheesecake, which comes highly recommended by UN staff, is every bit as delicious as foretold. A wide range of alcohol from around the world is also available.

Fun fact: there's no tax on your meal because the United Nations is located in international territory. Advance reservations are recommended, proper attire is required—jackets for men, no jeans, and no sneakers. A government-issued ID is necessary to pass through security. After your meal, you'll be escorted again with a final walk through the grand entrance hall.

BURGER JOINT AT LE PARKER MERIDIEN

119 West 56th Street, New York, NY 10019
- www.burgerjointny.com/56thstreet
- 212-708-7414
- Sunday to Thursday 11 am – 11:30 pm; Friday and Saturday
11 am – midnight
- Transport: F train/57th St
- Moderate

*Hidden
burger joint
in an upscale hotel*

It's been over a decade since Burger Joint first opened up in Le Parker Meridien hotel on 57th Street. By now it's considered one of the mainstays of New York City's burger scene, but the hidden spot still delivers, in part for its famous burgers but also for the juxtaposition between the divey 1970s interior and the posh monumentality of the marble Parker Meridien lobby. There's nothing that reveals Burger Joint's existence, tucked behind thick floor to ceiling velvet curtains, except for a neon burger sign (and the long lines) to denote what lies beyond.

Once inside, you'll be confronted with the scent of burgers, brownies and milkshakes wafting over from the open kitchen. Besides pitchers of Sam Adams beer, the aforementioned are the only items on the menu. Know what you want in advance, or you'll be yelled at and sent to the back of the line. If you freeze, just ask for "The Works" which puts everything on your burger: lettuce, tomato, onion, sliced pickles, mustard, ketchup, and mayo. The "666 Package" gets you a burger, fries and soda for $15.61 (exactly). Two butchers on staff spend most of their time just making burgers for the never-ending crowds, cooking them to that perfect texture. After you order, prepare to battle for a seat.

Because of its popularity, a visit to Burger Joint always shows a cross-section of the New York City population, plus the inevitable tourists. As Le Parker Meridien President Steven Pipes said in an interview with Eater, "What's great about our clientele is that you can't describe it. It crosses all social, economic, geographical possibilities."

Visually, the interior features vinyl booths, 1970s-era wood veneer paneling with sports and movie posters taped haphazardly, and no shortage of graffiti scribbles on the wall. In some ways, anachronism seems to be the theme throughout the hotel: a gothic-style bar within a neoclassical lobby, a Damien Hirst artwork contrasts with Roman arches. Fun fact: the lobby is actually a public atrium, part of 6½ Avenue, open until midnight every day. Follow 6½ Avenue to cross mid-block within buildings between 51st Street and 57th Street—it's even marked by street signs.

LANTERN'S KEEP

49 West 44th Street, New York, NY 10036
- 212-435-4287
- www.iroquoisny.com/lanternskeep
- Open Monday to Friday 5 pm – midnight; Saturday 6 pm – 1 am
- Transport: B, D, F, M and 7 trains/42nd St – Bryant Park
- Moderate

> *The Iroquois Hotel's little secret*

Open in the early 1900s, both the Algonquin and the Iroquois hotels exude the glamor of times past. Inside, the Algonquin has its famed Round Table restaurant, where Dorothy Parker gathered with editors of *Vanity Fair* and *The New Yorker*. But the Iroquois has a hidden little jewel box of a cocktail bar called Lantern's Keep. There's no sign for it, but in-the-know imbibers are aware that if the lantern affixed to the Iroquois's façade is lit, they can go inside and have a drink.

Lantern's Keep opened in 2011, but you wouldn't know it from the decor, which looks more like a Parisian Beaux-Arts salon than a New York bar. Chic black paneling contrasts with marble tables and Louis XIV chairs upholstered in powder blue velvet. Impressionist-style paintings of ballerinas adorn the walls. A fireplace adds a touch of elegance. In the corner, a tiny bar (the bartenders call it the cockpit) is equipped with everything needed to whip up craft cocktails.

The youthful head bartender John Ploeser came up through the ranks in his hometown of Madison, Wisconsin before moving to New York to join the opening staff of Perla in the West Village. There he met Theo Lieberman, then head bartender of Milk & Honey, who further trained him in the fine art of making classic cocktails. Along with Meaghan Dorman, Ploeser and his team designed the list of forty original cocktails, from the refreshing Regal Business (gin, grapefruit, honey, lime) to the boozy Double Barrel (rye, dry vermouth, sweet vermouth, angostura and orange bitters). Ploeser has a polite, Midwestern air that makes him instantly likeable and easy to talk to (an important quality in a bartender) and though he studied French literature, he loves the social aspect of bartending and feels at home behind the bar.

Much like the original Milk & Honey in Chinatown, Lantern's Keep is like a port of call in a cocktail wasteland. Though the neighborhood has some beautiful historic places, the New Yorkers who work in the surrounding banks and office buildings have few choices besides the ubiquitous Irish pubs and gems like Lantern's Keep, which are still few and far between. Since the bar opened, it has been a haven for post-work cocktails and a happy discovery for tourists staying at the hotel.

UNDERWEST DONUTS

638 West 47th Street, New York, NY 10036
- www.underwestdonuts.com
- 212-317-2359
- info@underwestdonuts.com
- Transport: C and E trains/50th St
- Affordable

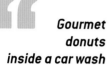

Gourmet donuts inside a car wash

Opened in December 2014 *inside* the 24-hour West Side Highway Car Wash, Underwest Donuts embodies in one swoop the evolving demographics and urban landscape of Hell's Kitchen. To pay for a car wash, drivers have to first walk a long hallway: on one side they can see their car getting washed, on the other side is the counter for Underwest Donuts, named after the nickname for the West Side Highway when it ran as an elevated roadway.

Owner Scott Levine comes from a background in fine dining, having worked at Union Square Events with Danny Meyer and at Chanterelle, with stints at Del Posto and Le Cirque. He originally wanted to open a bagel shop, hoping to reinvent the New York classic as Shake Shack did with the burger. But storefront rents were so prohibitive in the city, he was forced to reconsider his culinary angle. Meanwhile, Levine's father-in-law was looking for a food tenant for the West Side Car Wash, of which he is a co-owner. Seizing the real estate opportunity, Levine redeveloped the concept around the car wash. "I really love coffee, and I really have a sweet tooth," he says, and for a car wash, "coffee and donuts straight up makes sense."

Levine makes everything from scratch, applying a high-end approach to a mass-market classic. He taught himself how to make donuts and the experimentation pays off. One taste, and you'll erase every other prior conception you have of donuts. He wants them to be moist, and in some cases, "decadent" and indeed they are–somewhere between pastry and dessert. They're also somewhat smaller than the usual donut, making them less of a guilty pleasure.

Levine is constantly refining the textures and coming up with new flavors. He says, "If I'm going to call a donut a coconut lime donut, you better well be able to taste coconut and lime." There, he uses fresh lime juice and coconut milk to create the flavor. At the same time, he geeks out on the nutritional facts, making spreadsheets to understand the relationship between the flavors developed and the ingredients used. With flavors like espresso bean, halva (a Middle Eastern confection of ground sesame and honey), brown butter, dark chocolate, coco raspberry and cinnamon, it's hard to know where to start. The old fashioned donut is $1.50, the sugared donuts are powdered to order costing $1.75, and the glazed donuts are $2.50. There's coffee from Brooklyn Roasting Company along with espressos, cappuccinos and macchiatos.

The hours align with the car wash hours, opening at 6:30 am on weekdays and 7:30 am on Saturdays. Levine begins his day early at 2:30 am, making the glazed donuts first because they stay moist longer. During those early hours, he sees a lot of interesting stuff, he says. A regular occurrence: drunk partiers from the nearby clubs who desperately want donuts. They'll have to wait until opening.

WOMEN'S NATIONAL REPUBLICAN CLUB RESTAURANT AND PUB

3 West 51st Street, New York, NY 10017
• 212-582-5454
• www.wnrc.org/
• Open Monday to Friday, Saturdays seasonally to hotel guests only—check on ext. 2215 for hours/reservations
• Transport: B, D, F and M trains/47-50 Sts – Rockefeller Center
• Moderate

Founded by New York suffragists

The Women's National Republican Club is a gorgeous clubhouse built on the site of the former home of Andrew Carnegie next to Rockefeller Center. The club was founded by New York suffragists in 1921, but the organization moved into the current building in 1934 after the land was purchased from Carnegie. While it may exude the off-limits vibe of many Gilded Age clubs in New York City, the club is also a hotel with twenty-eight affordable guest rooms (in New York City at least) at about $250 per night.

The pub and restaurant located on level 2M is open to hotel guests. The menu includes bar bites like sliders and chicken wings, appetizers like crab cake and plantain-wrapped sea scallops, along with a large selection of salads, sandwiches, entrees, and desserts.

Though the architecture around the Rockefeller Center area has a tendency towards Art Deco and Modernism, the Women's National Republican Club followed the design tastes akin to the private clubs of the era: architect Frederic Rhinelander King designed the building in a neo-Georgian style both on the exterior and the interior.

According to the National Register of Historic Places, founder and first president Henrietta Wells Livermore "imagined the club as a major force in educating newly enfranchised women voters. From the beginning, the club offered lectures and seminars, and a School of Politics." But in a testament to its open mission, the club didn't have a president for the first fifteen years and was run by a collection of women.

Today, several different organizations also share the building, including a physics club and affiliate clubs including the Lambs Club, Squadron A Club, the Netherland Club and the Bond Club. Every Republican President of the United States has visited this building since it opened and the library, called the Calvin Coolidge Library, was donated by the wife of President Coolidge.

The spaces within the club, including grand ballrooms, can also be booked for private events. One room has a wonderful balcony offering a view of St. Patrick's Cathedral on Fifth Avenue and the hidden rooftop gardens at Rockefeller Center.

FREIGHT-ENTRANCE RESTAURANTS

El Sabroso: 265 West 37th Street
Arie's Cafe: 306 West 37th Street
• Open Monday to Friday
• Transport: 7, A, C and E trains/42nd St; 1, 2 and 3 trains/Penn Station
• Inexpensive

"

Hole in the wall countertops

There are few hidden places that keep their character over time in New York City without succumbing to the trendy crowd, but the hole-in-the-wall restaurants tucked away in Garment District freight entrances were created to cater to manufacturing workers and continue to serve them at cheap prices. Adding to the unique ambience, the doors constantly open and close for deliveries at the active loading docks. But don't expect anything more than a countertop and a few stools—the personal experience at these spots make them worth the adventure.

Self-proclaimed as "the best kept secret in the Garment District," Nick's Place, located on 39th Street, is the most well-known but it's also the least interesting in terms of both cuisine and space. More hidden options are El Sabroso at 265 West 37th Street and Arie's Café at 306 West 37th Street.

El Sabroso has been open for over twenty years with the same owner serving affordable Hispanic food. The nondescript sign outside reads "*Aqui ahorra y come bueno*" ("Here you will save and eat well"). Despite a full menu on the wall, your best bet is to ask Tony what he recommends for the day. For $6, you can get the stews that come with a plate of rice, beans, and lettuce. Don't forget to add some of the hot sauce, a secret family recipe Tony won't reveal. Empanadas with cheese or chicken are just $1 each.

There are five stools at the counter and a small wooden table if you want to eat in. Most patrons take out, but if you stay for a chat with Tony he might start to tell you of his trials and tribulations looking for a wife in this city.

One block over is Arie's Café, an unmarked Dominican restaurant. While El Sabroso is located in a spacious entrance, Arie's is down a very narrow corridor. This means that food lines compete with actual deliveries. Somehow though, Arie's manages to cram in nine countertop seats. The hallway is also shared by a knock-off DVD peddler, set up just in front of the kitchen.

You'll never be quite sure if what you ordered is what you actually received, but there's a good chance it'll be stewed goat, marinated overnight. $5 gets you the main course atop rice, beans, and plantains.

An added bonus: the tourists from nearby Times Square rarely venture into this neighborhood and it's a little too far for the Madison Avenue lunch crowd, meaning both the clientele and the restaurants stay true to how they've always been.

DIAMOND DISTRICT RESTAURANTS

Taam Tov 41 West 47th Street, 3rd floor
El Rincon del Sabor 74 West 47th Street, 4th floor
• Taam Tov open Monday to Thursday 10 am – 9 pm, Friday 10 am to
before Sabbath, Sunday 11 am – 6 pm
• El Rincon del Sabor open Monday to Thursday 11 am – 4 pm, Sunday
11 am – 3:30 pm
• Transport B, D, F and M trains/Rockefeller Center
• Moderate

Above
the world's largest
diamond district

It is estimated that over 90% of the diamonds that enter the United States come through New York City, the majority through one block on 47th Street. There are shops upon shops of diamond dealers, gold buyers, and jewelry polishers. Hawkers on the street aggressively seek buyers and sellers, and amidst these are men advertising two restaurants on the block—Taam Tov with Central Asian cuisine and El Rincon del Sabor, an Ecuadorian restaurant—both hidden on upper floors.

The cuisine choice makes sense for the main clientele, the 23,000 workers who make a living on the block. The Diamond District, formed in Midtown in the years before World War II, grew in importance during the war as Jewish diamond dealers fled to New York. Behind and above the façade of diamond stores on the ground floor are the Hispanic and Chinese laborers who set and polish the jewelry.

Taam Tov has been on 47th Street for over ten years, owned by a group of individuals from Israel and Uzbekistan. Enter through a narrow staircase, and pass the first and second floors. On the third floor, you'll first come across a takeout window, with delivery men on the stakeout for the next order. Just down the hall is the entrance to the restaurant. The glatt kosher food is Bukharian in origin, with specialties like Uzbek pilaf, beef stroganoff, and *bakhsh*. Also available are shish kebabs, steaks, lamb chops, traditional soups, and ten different types of salads. A must-have is the *lepeshka*, the Uzbek homemade bread paired with an order of *baba ganoush*. The food is delicious—a balance of simple ingredients packed with flavor.

El Rincon del Sabor is on the fourth floor, with an easy-to-miss sign high above the street. A visit here is more for the food than for the atmosphere. There's a simple counter showing the day's stews, behind which is a small kitchen. There are just nine tables and it gets crowded over lunch, with a constant flow of new customers plus delivery orders. The menu is different each day, with a traditional mix of rice dishes, stewed and grilled meats, shrimp ceviche and fried fish, listed in Spanish first, then English.

Despite the spartan decor, both El Rincon del Sabor and Taam Tov are places for leisurely lunches. The hidden nature of both spots ensure that the experience of eating in the Diamond District continues to reflect the unique ethnic breakdown that make up this dense business district.

BAR CENTRALE

324 West 46th Street, New York, NY
- 212-581-3030
- www.barcentralenyc.com
- Open daily 5 pm – late
- Transport: N, Q and R trains/49th St; C and E trains/50th St
- Moderate

> *Nitecap spot for Broadway stars*

Up a flight of steps and behind a nondescript townhouse door, Bar Centrale feels a world away from the hustle and bustle of the Theater District. Outside, chaos reigns, inside, the bar is a safe haven. Broadway actors come here for a nightcap after their shows, knowing they can count on the staff's discretion.

Bar Centrale is definitely not a period piece like Sardi's, Barbetta, and other longstanding spots in the neighborhood, but there are nods to the area's history throughout the space. When you first walk in and pass through a velvet curtain, you're face to face with a coat check manned by an attendant (quite rare these days). Black and white photos grace the walls, and a small TV above the bar plays old movies, like *Sabrina*. There are booths and black tables, one of which has ticket stubs and matchbooks under glass. Even the bathroom has blown-up black and white vintage photos of Times Square and nearby Hell's Kitchen. It's glamorous, but not showy; a bit retro, but not put-on. The whole place has an air of mystery—you never know who you might see.

The menu is equally distinguished but unfussy. There's wine, beer, and classic cocktails for people who don't need to look at a menu, but just order their Tanqueray Martini with a twist because that's how they always take their Martinis. Ask for one and the bartender will serve it in a small glass, with a mini carafe that keeps the rest of your drink on ice, so you never have to go through the agony of imbibing a warm cocktail. Bar fare includes classics like oysters, shrimp cocktails, and caviar, plus lobster quesadillas, vegetarian samosas, and Chinese dumplings. Service is courteous and attentive.

Speakeasies and hidden bars are relatively rare in Midtown. Perhaps because historically, development started downtown and slowly worked its way up. During Prohibition—when bars were forcibly driven underground—this area was relatively uncharted territory. Aside from Barbetta—the oldest restaurant in New York City continually run by the same family—this area was just developing in the early 20th century. It wasn't until 1973 that 46th Street came to be known as Restaurant Row, thanks to Mayor John Lindsay. The fact that Bar Centrale is hidden behind a townhouse façade lets actors come and go in peace, even while fans and paparazzi shuffle in and out of the other restaurants on the block.

MANHATTAN CRICKET CLUB

226 West 79th Street, New York, NY 10024
• 646-823-9252
• www.mccnewyork.com
• Open seven nights, 6 pm to late
• Transport: 1 train/79th St; B and C trains/81st St or Museum of Natural History
• Moderate

1870s apartment style bar

Hidden inside the Australian-themed restaurant Burke & Willis, the Manhattan Cricket Club is a rare Upper West Side speakeasy. Just pass the long bar and open the tufted green leather door. A wooden staircase will lead you to a 19th century-style gentlemen's club. Keeping with the Australian inspiration, the Manhattan Cricket Club is inspired by the colonial clubs of the old British Empire.

The narrow upstairs space, three rooms in succession, is designed to feel like a small apartment from the 1870s. The first room, with a small window, functions as a foyer replete with wooden coat rack. The gold wallpaper, which begins along the staircase and spreads into the rooms, has a layer of flocked black velvet. The main sitting area is lined with books by Dickens and Maupassant, along with cricket trophies and vintage photographs. Wood paneling and a mirrored ceiling complete the room, with a chandelier of glass sconces and a frayed Oriental carpet.

The bathrooms are cleverly hidden behind sliding doors that blend into the decor, whether behind the wallpaper or behind a mirrored wall. Even the toilets are vintage, but the real gem of the Manhattan Cricket Club is the row of private liquor lockers in the mirrored hallway, where members of the club can store the spirit or wine of their choosing. The club assists in acquiring the stock from anywhere around the world. While visits to the Manhattan Cricket Club are walk-in only for the public, members can make advance reservations.

The bar room has a tin ceiling, an exposed brick wall and more vintage colonial decor. Mixologist Greg Seider, who created cocktail menus for Mercer Kitchen and Minetta Tavern, helms the offerings at Manhattan Cricket Club with drinks inspired by the old empire outposts. There's a mix of exotic flavors and traditional elements—"Our menu is not deep, it's thoughtful," they say. As a humorous touch, the menu is dotted with quotes about alcohol by famous people: "I drink to make other people more interesting," said Hemingway.

There's a freshness to the cocktails here. A strawberry and hibiscus infused gin is topped with agave, fresh lime and grapefruit bitters. Smoked black pepper white truffle mist and garden tomato essence top off the Salt & Pepper cocktail made with potato vodka. Smoked cinnamon, cilantro, and lemongrass black pepper infusion appear in other cocktails, giving just an indication of the creativity of the offering. In addition, there's a solid selection of whiskeys, wines, beer, sparkling wines, and champagnes. Food like oysters and crab beignets can be ordered from the kitchen of Burke & Willis downstairs.

Far from the downtown cocktail craze, the Manhattan Cricket Club is able to maintain its welcoming, neighborhood feel. You won't find the cozy, intimate experience interrupted by undesirable crowds because it's simply too far from the fray, and its understated cool means it will always be a place to catch up with friends.

SALONS AT BRAZENHEAD BOOKS

Secret location
• www.brazenheadbooks.com
• Bookstore open by appointment

Unofficial speakeasy bookstore

Hidden somewhere on the Upper East Side, Brazenhead Books is an unofficial speakeasy bookstore built out of an old winding apartment. Its operator Michael Seidenberg embodies, in live form, what a "brazen head" is: a head cast in bronze or brass capable of answering any question. What's more, he's affable and fun, as evidenced by the empty wine bottles, whiskey bottles and filled ashtrays still scattered on a counter following a late-night salon. In fact, Seidenberg claims that he and his dog are characters in Jonathan Lethem's *Motherless Brooklyn*.

Walking into Brazenhead is like happening upon the collection of a master hoarder. Books are shelved floor to ceiling, on the back of doors, in the narrow entrance hallway and on top of desks. Those that don't fit are stacked precariously on the floor.

It was a neighbor that suggested the idea of converting Seidenberg's old apartment into a bookstore. Seidenberg hopes to recreate the feel of the bookstores he frequented in New York City during the 1970s. Operating under the radar, the only way to visit Brazenhead is through a phone number shared amongst patrons. There is a website now, with wonderful, whimsical illustrations by Farr Q. Daufeen, exactly as you might expect a literary haven to have. But there's no indication on it as to its location or how to visit. But try the old-school route perhaps: look up Seidenberg in the phone book. These days, he seems to answer enquiries through the website too.

Though it may not seem like it, there is a semblance of organization at Brazenhead, with sections like "Russian fiction," "mass paperbacks," "New York Letters," and "romance." The back room has rare and first editions for collectors. You'll even find other collectibles—a 1970s New York City subway map that we picked up, for example.

Even a visit during non-salon hours is turned into a conversation, as there's more here than just buying books. Salons take place every Tuesday, Thursday and Saturday with Tuesdays dedicated to poetry. There may be impromptu film screenings, projected onto the bookshelves. Drinks are imbibed with NPR playing in the background. Most importantly, there's

BAR AND DINING ROOM
AT THE SOCIETY OF ILLUSTRATORS

128 East 63rd Street, New York, NY 10065
- www.societyillustrators.org
- Museum open Tuesday 10 am – 8 pm, Wednesday to Friday
10 am – 5 pm, Saturday 12 pm – 4 pm. Sketch nights Tuesday and
Thursday 6:30 – 9:30 pm
- Monthly brunches and dinners open to the public
- Transport: F train/Lexington Av or 63rd St; 4, 5, 6, N, Q and R trains/
Lexington Av or 59th St

*Upper
East Side
arts club*

The Society of Illustrators is one of those hidden gems that even some of its neighbors don't realize exists—particularly the bar and dining room on the third floor of this Upper East Side club. Yet, the organization has been active since 1901 and in its current home, an 1875 carriage house, since 1935.

Though the Society of Illustrators is a membership-based club, it's open to the public every day the club is open because it's also a museum. In addition to a permanent collection of 1,800 works, the Society hosts special exhibitions throughout the year, weekly nude sketch nights, and themed sketch nights ranging from burlesque to boxing.

The Society's first monthly dinners in the early 20th century were attended by esteemed illustrators and personages like Mark Twain, Gloria Swanson, and N.C. Wyeth. The Cotton Club Band and Jimmy Durante performed here in the 1920s. The monthly brunches and dinners continue today in the dining room, with a charming historical bar, an outdoor patio and a rotating exhibition of artwork.

An original painting by Norman Rockwell, *The Christmas Coach*, was donated to the club by the artist himself in 1935 and hangs above the bar. In Rockwell's description of the painting, he writes, "This painting now hangs in the clubhouse of the Society of Illustrators, New York. The bartender, Ted Croslin, is well known to illustrators, who are so fond of him that when he went to war they gave him a dinner. He is not as dour as he looks."

At the time, the bar at the Society was on the fourth floor. In the 1950s, the bar on the third floor was created and the Rockwell painting moved there in 2008. Above hangs a wooden crest from the dining table of *LIFE Magazine* illustrator Charles Dana Gibson.

The dining room fare is headed by Chef Q, who is known for his challah bread banana brûlée french toast and banana maple walnut syrup. The $30 brunch comes with a full buffet, coffee, tea, and a Mimosa, Bellini or Bloody Mary cocktail. The dinner, also a buffet, is $50. There's no official drink menu but you can ask the bartender for whatever strikes your fancy. One of the off-menu specialty cocktails that has stuck around is "The F Train," consisting of organic cucumber vodka from Crop Earth, elderberry liqueur, lime juice, and pineapple juice.

GLASSERIE

95 Commercial Street, Brooklyn 11222
- 718-389-0640
- www.glasserienyc.com
- Open Monday to Friday 5:30 pm – 11:30 pm; Saturday and Sunday 10 am – 11 pm
- Transport: G train/Greenpoint Av
- Moderate

*Farm-to-table
fare in a former
glass factory*

On the northernmost tip of Brooklyn, the cavernous building that once housed the Gleason-Tiebout glass factory remained empty for years because the landlord refused to sacrifice the building's integrity for another deli. When Brooklyn resident Sarah Conklin explained that she wanted to restore the building to a version of what it once was, he was excited about the project. "As soon as I saw the courtyard, I was done," she says. However, this place is not exactly easy to find—the majority of the clientele have sought it out. Outside, only a neon green G marks the entrance.

The courtyard hidden in the back is paved with cobblestones and partly open to the sky. The building goes back much further than the entrance would have you believe. When it was a glass factory, from the 1870s to the 1930s, the workers would cart their wares through the courtyard to the back exit, which opens directly onto Newtown Creek. They then loaded the glass onto boats to be shipped. Now, the factory's enormous kiln door hangs in the courtyard and an original ceramic basin holds plants. "I'm genuinely charmed by this place," Conklin says. "There's an architectural value that's really untouched."

As she prepared to open Glasserie, Conklin spent months researching. She found antique etchings of the factory's fixtures—now hanging by the entrance—through the Corning Museum upstate. Vintage pendants, bare bulbs, and cut glass fixtures each emanate their own special glow. Above the bar hang two lights from Paris subway stations circa 1890, with Art Deco details on the sides. Poised around the room are copper pots from Lebanon and Saudi Arabia, handed down by Conklin's mother.

Conklin is half Lebanese, and felt that those flavors were underrepresented in New York City. To say, however, that Glasserie serves purely Lebanese or Middle Eastern food would be to simplify it. The menu changes daily, as per the fresh produce and meats available from farms in the New York area, including Brooklyn Grange's rooftop. The real emphasis is on seasonal ingredients and honoring the integrity of the flavors. Syrian cheese brushed with Za'atar might be served with heirloom tomatoes in the summer and pickled beets in the winter. The eclectic wine list emphasizes obscure wines from the Mediterranean, Slovenia, and Croatia. A simple gin & tonic takes on a new character with saffron simple syrup, which brightens the palate.

LUKSUS

615 Manhattan Avenue, Brooklyn, NY 11222
- 718-389-6034
- www.luksusnyc.com
- Open Tuesday to Sunday 6:30 pm – 9:30 pm, seatings every half hour
- Transport: G train/Greenpoint Av
- Expensive

Michelin-starred Scandinavian-style cuisine

Ten years ago, Greenpoint was the last place you'd expect to find an upscale restaurant with a $95 Nordic tasting menu—let alone one with a Michelin star. Getting people to brave the (universally bemoaned) G train to have dinner in this North Brooklyn enclave was near impossible. All of that is changing, and the tiny Luksus restaurant hidden behind the craft-beer bar Tørst is a part of that.

This spot—more of a tasting room than a full restaurant—still flies under the radar among the local crowd, who are likely to sip craft beer in wine glasses at Tørst without ever visiting it. Both are owned by the acclaimed chef Daniel Burns, an alum of Noma in Copenhagen and Momofuku. Both look like they'd be right at home in Copenhagen. Inside Tørst, light and dark wood on the walls, floors, tables, and chairs dominate the space. A white marble bar has twenty-one taps for craft beer, arranged from dark to light. Luksus is hidden behind a sliding door at the back of the bar, which many bar patrons never even notice.

You'll need a reservation to get into Luksus—not because that's a strict policy, but because it only seats twenty. There's only one row of tables lined up at a wooden bench that faces the open kitchen. Luksus chefs prep each dinner several hours ahead, and the food is flawless. "My time in Denmark was some of the most influential in my career," Burns says. "What I took from it was bright clean flavors, less ingredients but more focus on them so they shine." His seasonal tasting menus change every four to five weeks, but always include an *amuse-bouche*, a crudo course, a broth course, a main course, and a dessert. Diners might begin with a bite-size taste of cod head on *knakbrød*, a Danish flatbread. Vegetables and fruit from the farmers market at nearby McGolrick Park might show up in a dish of squab with salted plum purée.

Don't bother asking for a wine list; there's only beer, brought over from Tørst and carefully paired with each course. "I wanted to show people that beer is a legitimate beverage for pairing with food," Burns says. He has certainly succeeded: Luksus is the world's only Michelin-starred restaurant that doesn't serve wine.

NO NAME BAR

597 Manhattan Avenue, Brooklyn, NY 11222
• Open Sunday to Thursday 3 pm – 4 am, Friday and Saturday
12 pm – 4 am
• Transport: G train/Nassau Av
• Moderate

Like drinking on the Orient Express

The unmarked bar behind the burnt-wood façade of 597 Manhattan Avenue in Greenpoint not only lacks a name and a website, it doesn't even have a phone. "It might sound cliché, but I wanted to bring back a sense of discovery," says Jessica Lee Wertz, the bar's owner.

Visitors who manage to find this bar without a name will certainly feel transported. The only entrance marker is the antique bronze doorknocker shaped like a Chinese dragon. Push the heavy door open and you'll find yourself in a long, narrow bar that feels a bit like the Orient Express. Opposite the bar, a series of narrow benches with tiny tables are reminiscent of train cars. The whole space is outfitted in reclaimed wood with design elements inspired by China, Japan, and Morocco. Even the face of the bar is made of antique trunks. Wertz wanted to create a space that would seem reminiscent of a tavern at the end of the Silk Road.

Wertz has lived in the neighborhood for over ten years, but she spent much of her early life in Asia. She was born in Korea, grew up there and in Okinawa, Japan, and lived in Hong Kong after graduating. She worked in the food and beverage industry for many years before coming to Brooklyn and worked in a metal shop on North 14th and Wythe in Williamsburg. When the opportunity to get this space arose, she grabbed it. She did a lot of the renovations by hand, even cutting up and laying down the slate used for the bar top. She had help along the way from friends in the community, including Alyssa Abeyta (co-owner of Hotel Delmano), Alyssa's ex-husband Ray, and John McCormick (owner of St. Mazie).

When Wertz first opened the bar in 2010, she recognized everyone who came to drink there. Now, there are always new faces—a result of the neighborhood developing. But the bar definitely has its regulars. Perhaps it has gained so many loyal followers because it bridges the gap between the dive bars and the upscale cocktail bars in the neighborhood. It's the kind of place where you can order an Old Fashioned and your friend can have a Budweiser, and there's no judgment either way. Many chefs and servers from the surrounding restaurants come in for a nightcap, since No Name is one of the few bars around that stays open until 4 am every night.

As for the lack of a name, it was a bit of a running joke. As the yearlong renovation process came to a close, Wertz's partners kept goading her. She was having such a hard time coming up with a name for the place, she kept putting it off. She had the grand opening without naming the bar, and it's been referred to as the No Name Bar ever since.

SAINT VITUS

1120 Manhattan Avenue, Brooklyn, NY 11222
- www.saintvitusbar.com
- Open daily 6 pm – 4 am
- Transport: G train/Greenpoint Av
- Inexpensive

Brooklyn's hidden heavy metal bar

From the outside, with its unmarked black metal door, Saint Vitus might seem intimidating, especially if you go on one of the nights when there's a burly biker guarding the door. But as soon as you enter, you find yourself in a warm, enveloping space. Candles in red votive holders give the whole place a warm glow. When Arty Shepherd (a musician) and his partners (former bartenders at Matchless) secured this location, they set about rebuilding it from the ground up.

The place had been a plumbing school, and they wanted to make it look like a church. Look up and you'll immediately notice the stained-glass window depicting Jesus on the cross, found at the Brimfield Antiques Fair in Massachusetts.

Shepherd also brought back a church's wrought-iron votive holder. Behind the mahogany bar, they keep album covers and other offerings from the bands that play. Drink specials consisting of a beer and a shot are dubbed "the priest," "bishop," "el cardenal," and "pope." In the window, an upside-down cross made of duct tape was put up as a gag, but ended up staying because so many people like taking their photos with it.

"This place was built by bartenders and musicians," Shepherd says. They designed the bar to be very functional, and the back room has some of the best acoustics in the city. They have performances almost every night of the week, which rock and heavy metal fans come from all over to see. Nirvana members Dave Grohl and Krist Novoselic took the stage with Joan Jett and Kim Gordon for a secret show at two in the morning, after their Rock Hall tribute at the Barclays Center. Grohl left an autographed copy of *In Utero*, displayed proudly behind the bar. Secret shows like this happen often, only announced the day of, in order to keep the turnout under control. But anyone can stop by to have a drink and take in the atmosphere anytime.

CELLAR AT ST. MAZIE BAR & SUPPER CLUB

345 Grand Street, Brooklyn, NY 11211
- 718-384-4807
- www.stmazie.com
- Open daily 6 pm – 1 am
- Transport: L and G trains/Lorimer – Metropolitan
- Moderate

Dine in a haunted cellar

Poised on the edge of Grand Street in Williamsburg, just before it drops off onto the Brooklyn-Queens Expressway, St. Mazie Bar & Supper Club is in a rather obscure location, but it's well worth the walk. Cross the threshold and marble café tables flanked by potted palms welcome you in. The wooden ceiling is curved, like the side of a ship, with rotating ceiling fans. Behind the bar stands a genuine 1920s refrigerator salvaged from a Buddhist monastery upstate. Toward the back, which resembles an old train car, wooden panels from a courthouse hem in the long, curved, leather banquette with tables and cane chairs. An antique sign for "Uptown Local Trains" hangs above. On a small stage in the corner with an upright piano beside it, musicians play gypsy jazz, swing, and flamenco on alternating nights of the week.

Every detail was meticulously chosen by John McCormick, who has had a hand in the design of several vintage-inspired neighborhood staples, including Maison Premiere, Five Leaves, the No Name Bar, and his own Café Moto (co-owned by Bill Phelps). He christened this place St. Mazie in honor of Mazie—just an old lady who watched after the Bowery's drunkards, really—profiled by Joseph Mitchell in the *New Yorker* in 1940. Here, she's been elevated to sainthood.

You could easily settle into the corner booth with a cocktail like the Gypsy (gin, Dolin blanc, and maraschino liqueur) and a platter of oysters, but then you'd be missing the real fun downstairs. An easy-to-miss door across from the bar opens onto a staircase that descends to the cellar—and that's where you'll really feel transported.

The dimly lit, low-ceilinged room was carved out by Italian stonemasons in the 1880s and served as a speakeasy and gambling den during Prohibition. With antique portraits hanging on the stone walls, rough-hewn wooden tables, and a small bar in the corner, it has the feel of an Old World wine cellar, like the ancient dank bars in the Parisian Latin Quarter. When you stand there, with the Django Reinhardt guitar strands reverberating through the wooden beams up above, you feel the forbidden excitement the people who came here to drink illicitly must have felt. Back then, this was a working-class neighborhood full of Italians and Eastern European Jews. Today, the owners insist there are ghosts haunting the cellar.

When John and his wife Vannesa opened St. Mazie, they intended the cellar to be its own thing: a supper club operating under the name St. Charles Cellar.

They began serving a full menu focused on European comfort food, with favorites like roast chicken and slow-roasted porchetta with fresh herbs and spices. Though you can now get anything off the dinner menu upstairs in the bar, a meal in the cellar is a real treat.

HOTEL DELMANO

82 Berry Street, Brooklyn, NY 11211
- 718-387 1945
- www.hoteldelmano.com
- Open Monday to Thursday 5 pm – 2 am; Friday 5 pm – 3 am; Saturday 2 pm – 3 am; Sunday 2 pm – 2 am
- Transport: L train/Bedford Av
- Moderate

Old World sophistication in Williamsburg

Don't be misled by the name. Hotel Delmano isn't a hotel at all, though owners Michael Smart, Alyssa Abeyta, and Zeb Stuart were inspired by weathered hotel lobby bars. When they got their hands on this prime space on the corner of North 9th and Berry, they leapt at the chance to create a bar that they would want to hang out in. Their retro bar/music venue, Union Pool, opened in 2001 and at the time, Williamsburg's bars catered to a young, rowdy crowd. "I used to joke that people who graduate from Union Pool come to Hotel Delmano," Abeyta says. It takes a bit of effort to find though. The Berry Street entrance is gated off, so it looks like there's nothing there. The real entrance is around the corner on North 9th Street.

"We wanted a place where people could hang out and talk about poetry, music, or love, and not scream over the music," Smart explains. And so they built it. The name Delmano is a bastardization of *della mano*, Italian for "by hand." Over the course of a year, they renovated the space. They stripped the wallpaper, uncovering the original plaster and sealing it. Smart built the bar, the marble bistro tables, and some of the cabinetry. They sourced antique chandeliers, black and white photos, and an original 19th-century oil painting. A couple of rooms in back provide more intimate banquette seating under antique portraits.

"We built a place to escape reality and whisk yourself away," Smart says. Indeed, it's easy for locals and foreigners alike to feel swept away and yet familiar and comfortable. You'll find many goods by local purveyors: gin from Greenhook Ginsmiths, cheese from Murray's, and smoked fish from Acme. The wine list aims to surprise, straying away from conventional choices and showcasing small vineyards instead. Sherry is a personal passion of wine director Alex Alan, who lived in Spain. He has nothing but recommendations, and will be happy to help you choose from the twelve sherries served by the glass.

The cocktails—both house standards and seasonal drinks—are excellent. On the bar, you'll notice the glass bottles containing infusions prepared in-house. The head bartender works with the bar staff on new cocktail recipes. They collaborate, perfect their recipes, and present them to the owners. Sometimes people come in hoping to get a cocktail they had in the past, an amazing concoction with vanilla, apple, and cinnamon, let's say. The bartender can usually remember and recreate it, even if it's no longer on the menu.

LARRY LAWRENCE

295 Grand Street, Brooklyn, NY 11211
- 718-218-7866
- www.larrylawrencebar.com
- Open nightly 6 pm – 4 am
- Transport: L and G trains/Lorimer – Metropolitan
- Moderate

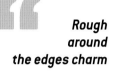

*Rough
around
the edges charm*

I f you look for 295 Grand Street, the first thing you'll see is an unwelcoming steel door with some faded graffiti. That's not the bar, but it has caused plenty of confusion. Presumably, enough people have tried to enter the landlord's apartment that the bar's owners had to tape up a sheet of paper printed with the name Larry Lawrence and some arrows. Enter and you'll find yourself in a long, bare hallway with nothing but cement walls and a couple of Edison bulbs. Open the door at the end of the hall and you'll be pleasantly surprised.

In many ways, Larry Lawrence is the kind of bar people expect in Williamsburg. It's long and dark, with an almost loft-like feel thanks to the high ceilings and glass balcony window. There's exposed brick, reclaimed wood, a backlit bar, and candlelit alcoves. The design is a bit raw, and the wooden benches are a bit clunky, but in a good way. As in a novel by Balzac, the setting reflects the characters who frequent it, especially the owners who built it. Because build it they did.

Back in the late '90s, when Williamsburg was still an industrial wasteland, Tatsuya lived there and worked in the service industry to put himself through art school. The way he tells it, he worked enough jobs in bars—saw how things were run—that he thought, "I could do that." When Tat and his business partner Ook decided to put their plan into action, they looked on the Lower East Side. When that didn't work out, Tat found the building on Craigslist. This was in 2003, and there was nothing else worth writing home about on Grand Street. They came in and the place was a raw, empty box. They were very into the idea of using what was there. The first thing they did was clean the brick. They built the front wall using wood from the landlord's barn upstate. They took extra pine beams from the ceiling and turned them into narrow tables. They built the benches and had the bar custom-made. It's simple, minimal, and very DIY.

The menu was a bit of an afterthought, though it has comments on each drink's origin. They serve classic cocktails like the Hemingway Daiquiri and Moscow Mule as well as beer on tap and wine. On a typical Friday night, you might find hipsters decked out in plaid guzzling pints, taking breaks to smoke up on the patio. Tat and Ook designed it with a big window looking into the bar, so you can be on the rooftop patio looking in and see the whole room laid out below—the ideal perspective.

MEXICO 2000 BODEGA

367 Broadway, Brooklyn, NY 11211
- 718-782-3797
- Open seven days a week 8:30 am – 10:30 pm
- Transport: J and M trains/Hewes St
- Inexpensive

"

Taco stand inside a bodega

Mexico 2000 is a hole-in-the-wall bodega in South Williamsburg under the elevated J-M-Z train tracks that gave Jay-Z his name. It's called Mexico 2000 simply because it was opened in the year 2000. But more than your typical neighborhood bodega, Mexico 2000 serves up tacos and other Mexican fare in the back of the shop and is a rare one where you can drink as well. Simply grab a can or bottle of beer from the sliding fridge doors, which are within arms length of the handful of tables. Many Mexican imports are available like Tecate, Modelo, Presidente, and Pacifico, along with tall boys of Pabst Blue Ribbon and cans of Four Loko. Go with a small group or sit with the regulars at the tables, watching telenovelas on the small TV.

Mexico 2000 made its mark on the New York City culinary map in 2012 when Alex Stupak of Empellón made a dish inspired by the *chilaquiles* from the bodega. But fans of Mexico 2000 had been going there for years, picking up American and Mexican basics like plantain chips, sweet breads, lotto tickets, toilet paper, and canned foods from rickety shelves, while grabbing cheap, authentic Mexican food from the back.

Besides the famous chilaquiles, there are tacos, burritos, chimichangas, tortas, huaraches, *sopes*, enchiladas, tostadas, and more, along with soups and stews favored by the staff that are off the menu.

The location of Mexico 2000 is one of its most interesting traits, right along the border of three distinct communities: the Hasidic Jewish neighborhood south of Broadway, encroaching gentrifiers from the north, and the existing Hispanic community. This means that the clientele at Mexico 2000 is a little slice of New York City's diversity. You might also see musicians emerge from a basement studio beneath a graffitied building right across the street.

There are actually two locations of Mexico 2000 on the same block in South Williamsburg now. The success of the tiny bodega led to an expansion two doors down into a formal restaurant, taking over a long shuttered space that was once a bizarre nail salon. Still, the taqueria in the tiny bodega remains active despite the expansion, and Brooklynites should be grateful. Anything in New York City that still feels homegrown and local, hole in the wall or not, should be held on to.

WYTHE HOTEL'S BASEMENT BAR

80 Wythe Avenue, Brooklyn, NY 11249
- 718-460-8000
- http://wythehotel.com
- Open for special events
- Transport: L train/Bedford Av
- Moderate

> *Bar hidden in Brooklyn's most famous hotel*

When the Wythe Hotel opened in 2012, it was a major event for Williamsburg—some might even say a turning point. The formerly industrial neighborhood on Brooklyn's waterfront had been gaining a reputation as New York's next up-and-coming area for about a decade already, but the addition of a luxury hotel stamped its place as a destination equally as desirable as Manhattan. What's more, the former cooperage, built in 1901, was renovated with a distinct Brooklyn sensibility. The design preserved the building's shell and incorporated materials reclaimed during the construction process. Custom Brooklyn toile wallpaper—a cheeky take on traditional toile—was created for the guest rooms, and local artists like Steve ESPO Powers and Tom Fruin created murals and the iconic Hotel sign, respectively. The result is a thoroughly modern seventy-room hotel that honors its industrial heritage and the neighborhood's artsy character.

For locals as well as tourists, the Wythe Hotel quickly became a place to see and be seen. Its ground-floor restaurant Reynard (a project of renowned Brooklyn restaurateur Andrew Tarlow) is a local favorite for upscale farm-to-table fare. Ides, the rooftop bar, boasts stunning views of the Manhattan skyline and regularly has a line of people waiting to get in.

Yet few people who come to dine at Reynard or drink at Ides realize that there's a much more intimate bar hidden in the hotel's basement. This bar doesn't have a name and it's only open for special events. Down there, the hotel's historic character is even more evident. Exposed brick walls and vaulted ceilings make you feel like you might be standing in the cooperage's storage space for wooden barrels. Instead of casks, there are bottles behind the bar, black leather booths, and marble café-style tables.

The little basement bar is attached to the screening room, which hosts film festivals and other private parties. A small, windowless dining room in the basement with exposed brick walls, long wooden tables, and little chandeliers, becomes the backdrop for the Wythe Hotel's annual Halloween party. Revelers typically spill over into the adjacent bar. Though you can't wander in off the street hoping to get a drink there, anyone can rent the space for a private event.

ZENKICHI

77 North 6th Street, Brooklyn, NY 11211
- 718-388-8985
- http://zenkichi.com
- Open Monday to Saturday 6 pm – midnight; Sunday 5:30 pm – 11:30 pm
- Transport: L train/Bedford Av
- Moderate

Tokyo-inspired hidden brasserie

The door to this very unique Japanese brasserie blends in with the tall wooden planks that adorn the façade, so even if you're looking, it takes a bit of effort to find the entrance. It's definitely not the kind of place you'd stumble into: most diners are seeking out a specific experience that's quite rare despite New York City's wealth of culinary options. Cross the threshold and you'll be in a dimly lit space with bamboo flanking a short hallway. A hostess will greet you at the host station and you'd better have a reservation. If you do, you'll be led upstairs through a maze of narrow hallways to your table.

There's no dining room the way Americans typically think of one. Instead, guests are seated in private booths: each one is divided from its neighbors by bamboo shades, so it's possible to hear the buzzing of other diners but not see them. Unlike in U.S. cities, in Tokyo, people aren't interested in sceney spots—privacy is prized more highly.

The intimate design was dreamed up by the owners Motoko Watanabe and her husband Shaul Margulies, who met in Tokyo in 2001. Homesick for her native Tokyo, which she and Margulies visited a few times a year, Watanabe decided that in order to get that quintessential Japanese brasserie experience in New York, she'd have to create it herself. The pared-back design allows guests to focus on the flavors of the food, the sake, and the pleasure of their companion's company.

Even beyond the design, Zenkichi is not your typical Americanized Japanese restaurant. You won't find any sushi here. You can order à la carte, but it's better to place your trust in the chefs, and go along for the ride. The *omakase* (eight-course chef's tasting menu) is ranked among the best in the city. The small plates emphasize the subtle and bold flavors of the season's best ingredients. Dishes are modern, but still traditional, and never veer into fusion territory. You might start with something familiar like miso soup, then quickly head into unfamiliar territory, with a plate of monkfish liver (prized in Japan as the foie gras of the sea) in a tangy citrus ponzu sauce. The Zenkichi salad (Motoko's favorite dish) is a delicious blend of silky homemade tofu, baby greens, and sesame dressing. There's crispy tempura, Washu beef steak with wasabi, and grilled black cod glazed in a yuzu citrus soy sauce. Your waiter can advise you on a sake pairing from the wide selection of all-natural premium sakes. They also have a vegetarian tasting menu and can cater to most dietary restrictions.

FEATHERWEIGHT

135 Graham Avenue, Brooklyn, NY 11206
- www.featherweightbk.com
- Open Sunday to Wednesday 7 pm – 2 am; Thursday to Saturday
  7 pm – 3 am
- Transport: L train/Montrose
- Moderate

Heavyweight cocktails in a former boxing studio

On the border of East Williamsburg and Bushwick, Featherweight is marked only by a small framed image of a white feather on a black door—recently added because the bar was so hidden people looking for it kept walking past it. Look up, however, and you'll see a huge black-and-white boxer painted onto the building.

The second floor once housed a boxing studio, and owners Johnny De Piper, Kathryn Weatherup and their partners took the building's past as their inspiration. First they opened the restaurant Sweet Science (an old boxing term), through which you can now get to Featherweight. But you have to go through a dimly lit alley—closed off at some point in the building's history.

De Piper speculates that the building was originally a home for a wealthy family, probably in the late 1800s. There was a fireplace where the backbar now stands. Back then, Williamsburg boomed with immigrants working in factories, like Havemeyer and Elder Sugar Refinery (which later became Domino), Brooklyn Flint Glass (which became Corning Ware), and Schaefer Brewery. Development was slower to come east, and this part of Brooklyn suffered from high crime rates until very recently. Heading east from Williamsburg, you can see the difference: huge housing projects tower over Broadway and atmospheric bars and restaurants are few and far between. That's why it's all the more surprising to find such a lovely little speakeasy here.

Featherweight is just one little room with a bar, three roomy mint-green booths, and some additional seating along the back wall and perched against a column. It's warm and inviting, though, with weathered tin on the walls and ceiling (found upstairs and installed here) exposed brick, dark wood, and a black velvet curtain guarding the entrance. Knick-knacks like boxing gloves, an antique birdcage, gold and porcelain peacock statuettes, and real peacock feathers line the shelves by the bar, along with bottles of hard liquor, amaros, chartreuses, and bitters.

These guys take their cocktails seriously. Protégés of Sasha Petraske, they follow the Milk & Honey school. The menu is composed of all-original cocktails offering inventive spins on the classics, like the Dirty Harry, a dirty Martini variation made with gin, house-infused olive brine, dry vermouth, and cracked black pepper. Homemade syrups enhance many of their drinks. Lada syrup, made with tomatillos, jalapeño, and coriander, goes into a cocktail made with gin, combier, and fresh lemon juice. Whatever you order, you can be sure it'll be good.

GOVINDA'S VEGETARIAN LUNCH

305 Schermerhorn Street, Brooklyn, NY 11217
- 718-875-6217
- www.radhagovindanyc.com/govindas
- Open Monday to Friday 12 pm – 3:30 pm
- Transport: A, C and G trains/Hoyt-Schermerhorn St
- Inexpensive

Hare Krishna's vegetarian delight

On the northern edge of Boerum Hill, Brooklyn, a large Hare Krishna temple stands as an anomaly, surrounded by dollar pizza joints and public welfare offices. Judging by the outside, you might never know that there's a vegetarian lunch canteen inside—a neighborhood spot unspoiled by guidebooks, most of which wouldn't be interested in such a modest, unglamorous place anyway.

But for Hindu devotees, neighborhood residents, and office workers, Govinda's is a convenient spot to get a cheap, healthy, and delicious vegetarian lunch in keeping with the Hare Krishna principles of nonviolence and service to god (Krishna) through vegetarianism. For the casual visitor, it's a window onto a small religious minority with a fascinating story.

Step inside and head down the stairs to the basement, where large round tables and metal chairs sit atop a clashing red and green linoleum floor. A small buffet station is set up at one end of the room, opposite a painting depicting the Hindu gods. The place looks like it has not been updated since its founding in 1982.

The decor is clearly not a priority, but that's not why you're here. You're here for the homemade samosas, roasted zucchini, tofu, and quinoa salad. The menu changes daily, and the cooks only serve fresh vegetarian food, both Indian and continental. A plate with your choice of three buffet items will leave you full for $6, and the proceeds support the temple.

The movement came to the United States in 1965, when 69-year-old A.C. Bhaktivedanta Swami Prabhupada arrived in Boston via freight ship to spread Lord Krishna's message in the West. Sent by his spiritual master in the holy land of Vrindavan, India, he had only $7 in change and a trunk of books on Krishna. He spoke at yoga studios, YMCAs, and bohemian artists' lofts, and often sat in parks playing a bongo drum and chanting the holy name of Krishna, gathering converts who believed in his teachings.

Govinda's canteen has been serving the community for the past six years. Before that, the staff only served meals after services, where devotees gather to chant the Hare Krishna Maha Mantra. Now, anyone is welcome.

WEATHER UP

589 Vanderbilt Avenue, Brooklyn, NY 11238
- 212-766-3202
- http://weatherupnyc.com
- Open daily 5:30 pm – 4 am
- Transport: 2, 3 and 4 trains/Bergen St
- Moderate

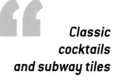

*Classic
cocktails
and subway tiles*

I f not for the gleaming white subway tiles covering the façade, you might never even wonder what's behind the door of this little place on busy Vanderbilt Avenue. Venture inside, past the velvet curtain, and you'll find yourself in a glowing little jewel box of a bar. Amazingly, the white subway tiles continue on the inside, completely covering the ceiling, just like in the Paris métro. Yet unlike a grimy subway station, the place is outfitted in dark wood, brown leather, a copper bar, and marble tables. A wall-hanging made from an old piano adorns the front corner. Custom light fixtures made from thin slabs of stone hang above the bar, and little votive candles give the room a warm glow.

A Brit by birth, Kathryn Weatherup has worked in the service industry since she was 14 years old. After studying architecture, she ended up a bartender in Paris before coming to New York, so the echoes of Parisian design may not be a coincidence. It was there that she met designer Matthew Maddy, who's responsible for the look of the bar, which he transformed from a rundown gospel church into another kind of house of worship. Though Weatherup had been working in bars and restaurants for years, it wasn't until she tasted a true Martini at Milk & Honey that she was finally bitten by the cocktail bug. Inspired by Sasha Petraske's return to the old-school way of making classic cocktails, she opened this little place near Prospect Park.

Petraske trained the staff, and it shows. Behind the bar, oranges, lemons, and limes sit in wire baskets, waiting to be pressed and blended with spirits and amaros. The short but sweet cocktail menu contains ten drinks—takes on the classics—but Weather Up's bartenders have the full repertoire of classic cocktails in their heads. Order a Vieux Carré (rye, cognac, vermouth, Bénédictine, bitters, and lemon) and you won't be disappointed. Try the Sir & Madam (gin, grapefruit juice, lemon juice, simple syrup, Peychaud's bitters, and sea salt) and you might just discover your new favorite drink. Should you be in the mood for something stronger, there's an absinthe fountain on the bar. You wouldn't be the first in this place to order yours on a drip. The bartenders, like Ben Curtis, are incredibly knowledgeable and friendly.

When the place opened in 2008, there were only a couple of other bars between here and Prospect Park. The formerly rough neighborhood has been changing steadily, and with the influx of more young professionals, Weather Up has gained a devoted group of regulars.

DUTCH KILLS

27-24 Jackson Avenue, Long Island City, New York, NY 10017
- 718-383-2724
- www.dutchkillsbar.com
- Open seven days a week 5 pm – 2 am
- Transport: E, M and R trains/Queens Plaza; E, M, 7 and G trains/Court St
- Moderate

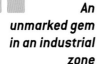

An unmarked gem in an industrial zone

In a nondescript two-floor brick building between a transmission shop and a taxi lot, Dutch Kills is an unmarked gem, save for a neon BAR sign and a plywood sign denoting "Blissville Kitchen." The area in Long Island City, formerly a forgotten industrial stretch off the Queensboro Bridge, is undergoing a transformation. Interspersed amidst the auto repair shops and taxi services are new high-rise glass rentals and condos. But this bar, opened in 2009, predated much of the gentrification taking place, distinguishing itself from other speakeasies through its comprehensive liquor selection and use of fresh ingredients in a cocktail menu that appeals to those who enjoy spirits.

Despite nearby development, walking into Dutch Kills still feels like entering a long-lost world. You'll first encounter the main seating area with private wooden booths that seat anywhere from two to six, divided from each other by red curtains. The experience at Dutch Kills is about intimacy and the architecture reflects that. The same wood paneling on the wall continues onto the low ceiling, giving the space a real, old-school tavern feel. You'd never guess that the same space used to be a fishmonger's office and cold-storage facility.

In the lofty back room is a long wooden bar with a silver cash register. The bar stools are circular and spin, like in a New York luncheonette but upgraded. A small skylight lets in a little daylight in the otherwise dim space. The numerous bottles behind the bar are organized by type, with all the classics plus absinthe, amaros, and mezcal.

The vibe at Dutch Kills has always been deliberately divey and fun, functioning simultaneously as a neighborhood bar for residents and a destination for others. The bar room is decorated with vintage memorabilia including a jukebox, money from Europe, religious art and old advertisements. Mixed in are modern-day additions, like the menu served at the birthday of one of Dutch Kills' long-time patrons. Mismatched light fixtures hang from the ceiling, but work with the eclectic decor.

The drink menu offers cocktails directly descended from New York City classics from the 1880s to the 1940s. There's an offering of hot drinks too, including Hot Toddy, Irish Coffee, and Mulled Cider. Dutch Kills bartenders can also make drinks based on your preferences or, for the curious, let them do their magic. On a visit pay attention to the glasses: the round cocktail coupes are often used in bars in Sasha Petraske's group and predate triangular Martini glasses. Water is served in Art Deco silver julep cups with metal straws.

And the name Dutch Kills? The kills, meaning a channel or creek in Dutch, refer to the former waterways of the area that have long been paved over. Still, they remain in various nomenclature around Long Island City, and in this wonderful hidden bar on an industrial stretch of Jackson Avenue.

GANESH TEMPLE CANTEEN

45-47 Bowne Street, New York, NY 11355
- 718-460-8484
- www.nyganeshtemplecanteen.com
- Open seven days a week 8:30 am – 9 pm
- Transport: 7 and 7X trains/Flushing – Main St
- Inexpensive

*Dosas
for the gods*

Across from a row of single-family houses in Flushing is a large building with an entrance so intricately carved, it looks straight from a temple in India. The Ganesh Temple, as it's colloquially known, was founded in 1970 with the current building dating from 1977. Its official name is the Hindu Temple Society of North America, named such because when founded in 1970 it was the first and only traditional Hindu temple in the country.

But the story goes back much further to America's colonial period. Predating the Bill of Rights, a document known as the Flushing Remonstrance was signed by Flushing settlers in protest of Dutch persecution of Quakers, extending "the law of love, peace and liberty," beyond Christians to all faiths and backgrounds. Flushing farmer John Bowne soon welcomed Quakers to meet at his house, which still stands. More than 350 years later, this same street, named after Bowne, now includes a synagogue, a Sikh gurdwara, a Chinese church, the Ganesh temple, and another Hindu temple.

The Ganesh temple is "permanently consecrated," meaning there's a permanent staff of priests that manage the holy statues. The stone deities on the exterior of the building were reconsecrated in 2009 with an impressive nearly week-long ritual. A cow and a 37-year-old elephant were part of the festivities–an homage to Ganesha, the elephant-headed god.

But downstairs is a canteen serving up dosas, masalas, and mango lassi so good it warranted a visit from Anthony Bourdain. There are seventeen variations of dosas, and an additional four varieties available only on weekends. A nearby Hindu resident says that the canteen was started to compete with the Dosa Hutt next door, but the official story from the temple president is that the canteen got its start when a chef was hired in 1993 to cook *naivedyams* (food offerings) for the gods, but was soon cooking for the worshippers too.

The all-vegetarian canteen is open seven days a week from morning until night with Ganesha in gold overseeing the basement dining space. Afterwards grab some desserts at the sweets shop in the Swaminarayan Hindu temple just down the street or explore the Golden Mall, a subterranean Chinese food court also in Flushing.

GOLDEN MALL FOOD COURT

41-28 Main Street, Flushing, NY 11355
- Open seven days a week
- Transport: 7 and 7X trains/Flushing – Main St
- Inexpensive

"

Underground
Chinese food court

Don't let the word "shopping" fool you when you go looking for the Golden Mall just a few blocks from the Flushing-Main Street subway station. You might be easily confused by the offerings of the Golden *Shopping* Mall above, a mishmosh of knock-off DVD shops, computer repair joints, hair salons and storefront restaurants. But what you're looking for is the Golden Mall (sans "shopping"), an underground food court of traditional Chinese food.

Open a nondescript set of double doors and go down a set of aging stairs to be confronted with a density of food stalls, scents, and noises that will transport you straight out of New York City. Yes, Anthony Bourdain may have ventured down here before you but the Golden Mall has unabashedly refused to upgrade despite the attention. The floors are grungy, mismatched and straight-up dirty on rainy days, and it's cramped. Yet, only the locals seem to venture beyond the most famous stands like Xi-an Famous Foods and Lan-Zhou Hand Pulled Noodles, but they're all worth a try.

After you order (and hear your dish yelled out in various dialects of Chinese), you'll be sitting on stools wherever you can find space–a countertop or a metal communal table that's piled with restaurant supplies. In the back area, two restaurants have booth seating.

Here's a rundown of what you should try in this cacophonic, culinary world below ground, and luckily there seems to be a self-regulated system of competition: every stall offers something a little different. Some spots don't have English names, but thanks to the media attention and new patrons, most of the menus have been updated with English translations and photographs of the food to make ordering easier than before.

For the spicy inclined, Xi-an Famous Foods is still a must-try, particularly because this is the original location of the now expanded franchise. Get the lamb cumin burger or one of the hand pulled noodle dishes. Lan-Zhou Hand Pulled Noodles next door has at least twenty-six versions of pulled noodles on the menu, and the best part is watching the worker slam the dough, twist it in the air, and turn it into thin strands within seconds. Order with meats like ox-tail, tripe, seafood, roast duck, intestine, and cattle tendon.

Tianjin Homemade Dumplings offers dumplings as cheap as $4 for twelve pieces, this after a $1 price increase in December 2014. The classics–pork dumplings with chives, cabbage or dill–and variations of chicken, beef and lamb dumplings are on the menu. But you can also make your own, choosing

FINBACK BREWERY TASTING ROOM

7801 77th Avenue, Queens, NY 11385
- info@finbackbrewery.com
- www.finbackbrewery.com
- Open Thursday and Friday 4 pm – 9 pm; Saturday 1 pm – 8 pm; Sunday 1 pm – 7 pm
- Transport: L and M trains/Myrtle – Wykoff, then Q55 bus
- Moderate

Inventive beers in Queens

This gem of a tasting room is worth the trek to Glendale, Queens and getting there is part of the adventure. From Manhattan you take the L or the M train to the Myrtle – Wyckoff station at the literal border of Brooklyn and Queens, transfer to the Q55 bus and then walk through a residential neighborhood in Glendale. Suddenly on 77th Avenue, you'll encounter some warehouses. In the winter, the garage doors will all be closed and the only hint that something is going on may be the "Yes, we're open!" sign taped to one of the unmarked doors.

For the (epi)curious, opening this particular door on the otherwise uniform industrial block will lead to a beautifully designed tasting room and bar retrofitted into the loading dock of Finback Brewery. The bar is lined with bright silver metal stools and the wooden tables and benches in the main seating area were handmade by the Finback team. The wooden tap handles, each stamped with the Finback logo, are built into a marble wall. Above, a mirror doubles as a menu where they write and cross out brews as they're available. From the bar, you can see right into the brewery itself, with its mash tanks and grain silos. Sometimes the staff zips through the tasting room on skateboards, carrying empty plastic barrels.

Owners Basil Lee and Kevin Stafford began as home brewers, and it's evident in the inventive mix of flavors that are in Finback beers. If you're looking for rich, unique flavors, this is the brewery for you–with sour beers and others flavored with the likes of jalapeño, coconut, mango, and plum. The Double Sess(ion) is brewed with Szechuan peppercorn, chamomile, and ginger: a great choice as a summer beer or for those that like beers less hoppy. The Fort Tildenist beer is brewed with green tea and lemon zest. Finback beers have clever names like Coasted Toconut, Cat Love, and Plumb & Proper, along with seasonal beers and Finback IPA that's always on tap.

In the back rooms of the warehouse, Finback is aging beer in bourbon, whiskey, and wine barrels. In late 2014, Finback released a barrel-aged BQE beer brewed with cocoa nibs from Mast Brothers Chocolate and coffee from Native Coffee Roasters in Queens, along with another barrel-aged beer called Smoke Detection.

Beers are currently only available on tap at bars in the greater New York City area and visiting the Finback Brewery tasting room is a great opportunity to hear directly from the team that heads up this small local business. Plus, there's always free popcorn from the vintage machine in the corner.

DINNER LAB

Members Supper Club
- www.dinnerlab.com
- Two to three events in NYC per week
- Moderate

Supper club in unique locations

Among the supper clubs in New York City, Dinner Lab occupies a unique niche for diners also interested in hard-to-access locations. Dinner Lab has hosted suppers on a helipad, in a motorcycle dealership, in the abandoned South Street Seaport Mall food court and in a church, all with top chefs. The locations are used once only and dinners get sold out within minutes.

Though Dinner Lab is in over twenty cities in the United States, it began simply among a group of friends in New Orleans in August of 2012. It was originally a late-night dining concept aiming to showcase different ethnic cuisines to a city heavily influenced by southern and Cajun food. The first location was a decrepit old brothel and an Eventbrite glitch caused 200 tickets to be sold instead of the forty intended. But scrappy is what Dinner Lab was and still is, and they managed to serve everyone.

Now, Dinner Lab aims to bring strangers around a long communal table, showcasing cuisine by great chefs from different ethnic backgrounds. These chefs, often the sous chefs and chefs de cuisine of famous New York City restaurants, use their nights off to get creative. New York City was the fourth city in Dinner Lab's expansion, with Austin and Nashville getting off the ground after New Orleans. But founder Brian Bordainick is from the New York area and was drawn back here.

In terms of finding locations, much of it is done by cold calling and sheer determination, the old-school way. Sometimes they'll pass a space on the street and find it interesting, other places are locations under construction that haven't opened yet.

The group of friends who started at Dinner Lab met getting their MBAs at Tulane and many parts of the business reflect their business-savvy start-up nature. Their unique membership model, with a yearly fee of $175, covers the operational costs of the company with its core team based in New Orleans. Local teams execute the events in each city, with one person on operations, and one in charge of food. This keeps prices affordable, with the ticket revenue going entirely to the dinners. Instead of going the venture capital route, Dinner Lab sought crowd-sourced funding from its membership base.

Each dinner has two seatings of sixty people each, so it's a large affair. 80% of the prep work is done in a kitchen off-site, but the last 20% is done in the same room as the diners so they can see the finishing touches. Inspired by requests from chefs wanting to know how they did, guests write feedback on cards, rating the courses, the service and the venue.

Joining can be through referral from a current member or by simply signing up on the website. Memberships open over the course of the year for set periods of time, particularly around holidays and press pushes, but you can always sign up on the waiting list.

EATWITH SUPPER CLUBS

Locations all over New York City
- www.eatwith.com
- Hours vary
- Price varies

Connecting people to creative hosts

As far as alternative dining goes, supper clubs are the ultimate experience. Secret supper clubs have probably been occurring since the earliest days of the city's history. In a way, they are the simplest, most basic form of restaurant. You go to someone's home and you exchange money for a meal. Yet, for many who want this type of experience, it's not easy to figure out where to go. So what is a supper club exactly?

First, it's not a restaurant: it takes place in a residence, usually with the host acting as chef, server, and busboy. It's not a dinner party: money is exchanged, and the host and guests are often meeting each other for the first time. Before the internet, you had to get an invitation by word of mouth. EatWith, a website that connects hosts to prospective guests, has made the whole experience much more accessible.

For people like Ai, who regularly hosts secret Japanese supper clubs with her husband Matt through EatWith, it's a chance to meet people of all different walks of life. They began throwing dinners for friends at first, and word got out that Ai cooks the kind of incredible Japanese food you won't find in a restaurant. When you walk into Ai's Williamsburg loft, you're immediately struck by what an incredible space it is. Plants climb the walls and hang down from the two-story-high ceiling. A vintage sofa defines the living room area. Off to the left, a stage displays bikes, salvaged windows, and lumber. By the stairs that lead up to the bedroom, shelves are stocked with dry ingredients in glass jars and bottles of liquor and bitters for mixing cocktails. The tiny open kitchen is crammed with every tool a professional chef could dream of. The centerpiece is the large grandmother-style dining table with mismatched vintage chairs all around.

Each supper club is different—some have menus, and some don't. Ai serves a seven-course vegetarian/pescatarian tasting menu, and she announces each dish as it's served. Most of the vegetables she uses are organic, bought at farmers markets or picked from her rooftop garden. Eating one of her meals, you might be shocked that she's not a professionally trained chef. That's one of the greatest strengths of the supper club: it's a format that allows both professional and home chefs (many of whom work unrelated day jobs) to explore, hone their skills, and share their love of food with strangers. The people who attend these secret supper clubs tend to be a self-selecting group—foodies—so around the table, guests have the chance to find an incredible camaraderie with like-minded individuals.

HOME COOKED MEALS WITH FEASTLY

Locations all over New York City
- www.eatfeastly.com
- Hours vary
- Price varies

Dinner in a Bed-Stuy bodega

When was the last time you had a home-cooked Togolese dinner inside a bodega after hours with a group of strangers and a DJ? The "WOÉZŌ Comfort" meal is one of the offerings on Feastly, an online platform that aims to reintroduce the home-cooked meal, connecting adventurous eaters with local cooks. The WOÉZŌ dinner (pronounced "way-zoh"), cooked by Peace Corps alum Mitch Bloom, takes place in Bed-Stuy Fresh and Local, a grocery store run by neighborhood couple Dylan Ricards and Sheila Akbar. The produce gets pushed to the side and a long communal table is set up just in front of the door. The guests who don't fit on the benches sit on produce crates, a surprisingly sturdy option that makes sense when you discover that Dylan and Sheila built out the homey bodega themselves. The shelves are made of discarded doors that came directly from their nearby apartment building when it got renovated.

More than just a dinner, WOÉZŌ becomes a way of life as Mitch convincingly demonstrates. The group of fifteen guests practice a Togolese greeting that should be responded to with "*Yoooooo,*" collectively before the dinner starts. Throughout the four-course meal, Mitch tells exuberantly of his two-year experience as a volunteer in a village in Togo. He learned this oeuvre of Togolese dishes from his next-door neighbor and her husband, every evening under the stars. Mitch has a Bachelor's degree in nutrition and a Master degree in food initiatives from New York University, so the partnership with Bed-Stuy Fresh and Local, which brings fresh, healthy offerings to a previously underserved area, is a good fit.

As Mitch says, he hopes to bring people to a remote corner of the world through its food. In fact, the dinner is infused with food items with cultural importance in Togo, like the beer of choice, Guinness (pronounced "*ghee-niss*"), boxed wine and Johnny Walker Black. At the same time, the dinner has a New York flavor too. In Togo, the whiskey is reserved for the most important guests, but here Mitch hands out small glass cups and pours everyone a shot. The Togolese Bissap cocktail of hibiscus tea is sweetened with maple syrup from the Hudson Valley, mixed with gin from the New York Distilling Company. The delicious *yovo* salad is made of a half avocado smothered in roasted sweet corn, red onion, and steamed dice beats, topped with cilantro and homemade sriracha. *Yovo* is Togolese for "foreigners" and as Bloom describes, "Although all the ingredients can be found in Togo, it's probably only a yovo that would make a salad like this."

The main course is a staple the Togolese call *la pâte*, West African smooth polenta with ginger-stewed okra and onions, topped with a choice of braised beef or garlic-sautéed oyster options (or both). Bloom explains that *la pâte* is typically eaten using the right hand. Next is the *koliko*, white yam fries with a ginger gazpacho sauce made with heirloom tomato puree, ginger, onion, and spices. The last course is a plate of tropical fruits and dark chocolates.

Throughout the night, DJ Temisphere spins in the corner. A warm glow emanates from the large storefront windows (with a central stained-glass piece) onto the otherwise quiet, residential streets of the Bedford-Stuyvesant neighborhood while a microcosm of New York mixes inside discovering a whole new culinary world. The WOÉZŌ Togolese Supperclub is just one of many offerings on the Feastly platform.

PLACEINVADERS

Various locations, supper club
- x.placeinvaders.co/
- Takes place monthly

W ith an adorable Invader icon sporting a chef hat, wine glass, and fork, PlaceInvaders is a supper club that takes over unique apartments in New York City for supper clubs and boozy brunches.

> **Voyeuristic meals in someone else's apartment**

There have been cocktails in an abandoned penthouse on the Upper East Side, a Maine-inspired meal featuring moose meat (which is illegal to buy) in an industrial loft, and a dinner in a Lower East Side home filled with taxidermy. Founders Katie Smith-Adair and Hagan Blount share a passion for cooking and living well in the city.

PlaceInvaders aims to open New Yorkers to a new type of urban experience and offers a more creative nightlife option than a bar or restaurant. The events are kept small and intimate, from eight to thirty guests, to mimic a dinner party "full of interesting people you'd like to know," says Katie. Hagan does the cooking, while Katie makes the cocktails and mingles with the guests.

When PlaceInvaders first started in 2014, the dinners were invite-only and guests received secret codes in batches. Locations, which are still only given last minute, were sent by Snapchat to ensure there was no paper trail. But they're officially a company now, so they can finally reveal their names and have a public Instagram account.

At a recent brunch, guests ventured onto an industrial block near the Navy Yard, home to things as diverse as the street art Pandemic Gallery, a controversial private Rabbinical college in a century-old warehouse, a kickboxing school, and a dry-cleaning headquarters. The entrance was easy to miss, with street numbers not consistently labeled. To get in, guests had to call a phone number and listen for a door with a faint buzzing noise.

Walking up wooden staircases worn down and bowed with time, they entered an apartment owned by a fashion merchandiser with flowing daylight, industrial exposed brick walls, and views of a Brooklyn rarely showcased. Large-format modern art hung on the walls and a small, elevated hideout was built into the space. A long communal table was set up with candles and a menu on each plate. For amateur chefs, the meal was nothing short of gourmet, including saffron oysters, "Beermosas," (the brunch drink of choice), and a "Big Game Pot Pie" of moose meat.

While PlaceInvaders is rooted in the voyeuristic pleasure of dining in someone else's apartment, the food has the essence of a couple cooking for the love of the cuisine. Repeat diners have become friends and hugs are not an uncommon sight as guests arrive and leave. Sign up on the PlaceInvaders website to get notified for upcoming events.

SALVAGE SUPPERCLUB

- Sign up at salvagesupperclub@gmail.com
- Dinners take place every three to four months
- Price varies

*Dinner
in a dumpster*

A few times a year, New Yorkers may come across a dinner party inside a dumpster. While at first glance, it may seem like yet another "hipster" pop-up, the Salvage Supperclub is far from that. It's a dinner series with a mission: to change the way people see food waste. Using expired and imperfect foods donated by local farms, restaurants and food co-ops, a gourmet multi-course meal is created by a chef and the proceeds are donated to food-related non-profits like City Harvest and Culinary Corps.

Founder Joshua Treuhaft started the supper club as a project for his thesis at the Design for Social Innovation program at the School of Visual Arts in New York City. He had always been passionate about food waste and started tackling how to get more residents to compost. But with slow traction, he realized that people are simply (and understandably) not excited about the end product of food waste. Turning everything around, Joshua began to target a more exciting stage of food consumption—turning food that's on its way to the trash into something beautiful to eat. Joshua hopes that the Salvage Supperclub will change the way people shop, look at food, and increase their knowledge of the life cycle of the products we consume. Just because the official expiration date has passed or because fruit is bruised doesn't mean it's not edible—and the supper club can teach you how to make that call.

After executing a few prototypes while at the School of Visual Arts, the first official Salvage Supperclub took place on the Gowanus Canal at the headquarters of Build it Green. Joshua retrofitted the dumpster himself, building custom Shaker furniture that was later sold by Built it Green. The next few dinners took place right on the street in Williamsburg and Prospect Heights in Brooklyn—with sixteen diners inside the dumpster.

The dinners are currently cooked by chef Celia Lam of the National Gourmet Institute, an early partner in Salvage Supperclub. Joshua pitched the institute the idea while in school with renderings and the organization immediately identified with it. With the constraints of using discarded foods, menu planning can be tricky. It takes around seven to ten days before the dinners to gather the raw ingredients and preserve them using different methods if needed. The dumpsters that are rented come with permits to park on the street, but in New York state it isn't legal to have an open container on a public sidewalk so cocktail hour takes place in an apartment above.

In the winter months, the outside dumpster locations are not feasible so the Salvage Supperclub moves into galleries and other indoor spots. There's no dumpster for those events, but there are panel discussions to round out the programming.

HONORABLE WILLIAM WALL CLUBHOUSE

- www.myc.org
- Open May to October; Dates and hours vary
- Departs from Pier 25 in Manhattan and Liberty Harbor Marina, Jersey City next to Surf City Restaurant
- Affordable

> **Floating club in New York Harbor**

The Honorable William Wall (aka the "Willy Wall") is the floating clubhouse of the Manhattan Yacht Club, anchored in the New York harbor just near Ellis Island. The open air bar has incredible views of downtown Manhattan and the Statue of Liberty (and neighboring Brooklyn and New Jersey, of course). Indeed, the clubhouse was designed specifically for taking in the sailboat races and you'll notice it is more of a viewing platform and barge rather than a sleek yacht. To get to the William Wall, you take the Admiral's Launch, a United States Coast Guard certified vintage motorboat from either Pier 25 in Manhattan or Liberty Harbor Marina in Jersey City (before 2015, it left from North Cove Marina in Battery Park). The red-hulled boat fits 40 comfortably.

The secret here is that you don't have to be a member of the club to experience the clubhouse: it's simply an $18 roundtrip launch fee, payable online. You can also just wait standby starting at 7:30 pm if tickets are sold out. Manhattan Sailing Club members get to go the front of the line, but that's usually not an issue for the 149-person capacity clubhouse except during peak periods.

The drinks are affordable and the offering is straightforward because the experience is ostensibly the races. Wine, beer, liquor and standard mixed drinks are available–served in plastic cups–but no cocktails. The chill factor is accentuated by the fact that you can bring your own picnics, or order food from Surf City in Jersey City, which gets brought to the clubhouse by the launch boat. The races begin at a buoy near the William Wall, go up the Hudson River and back, turn around in the cove behind the clubhouse, and return to the same starting point.

The first level of the William Wall is the formal clubhouse, a wood-beamed space outfitted with club chairs and a built in bar. Though this space was once exclusive to club members, it is now open to the general public as well. Here you will find memorabilia of the club's history and a small library. Framed is a letter from the Yacht Club of Monaco designating the Manhattan Sailing Club as the first ambassador of the Spirit of Tuiga Club, presided over by HSH Prince Albert II of Monaco. But the open-air top level, with the central bar, is where the action is.

And who is William Wall, you may ask? By all accounts he was rather "honorable," serving as a U.S. Congressman during the Civil War, consulted on by Abraham Lincoln in regards to the use of the Brooklyn Navy Yard. Born in Philadelphia, Wall was trained as a ropemaker and set up his own

Born in Philadelphia, Wall was trained as a ropemaker and set up his own business in Williamsburg in the 1820s, where he became a key figure in local government.

Getting out on the water, especially during the summer in New York City, is always a special treat, and the Honorable William Wall is one of the most affordable and unique ways to do that.

ALPHABETICAL INDEX

NOTES

Acknowledgements

We would like to thank all the friends who joined us on our explorations and the many bartenders, chefs, and proprietors who shared their insights and expertise.
Cheers!

Photography credits:

All photographs by **Augustin Pasquet** and **Michelle Young** except the photo of Salvage Supperclub (taken by Tanya Bhandari).

Map **Cyrille Suss** - Layout design: **Roland Deloi** - Layout: **Stéphanie Benoit** - Proofreading: **Caroline Lawrence** and **Kimberly Bess**

© **JONGLEZ 2015**

Registration of copyright: September 2015 – Edition: 01

ISBN: 978-2-36195-133-7

Printed in China by Toppan Leefung Pte. Ltd